Whispers of Faith

Young Friends
share their experiences of Quakerism

Edited, with chapter prefaces and notes, by
W. Geoffrey Black, P. Zion Klos, Claire Reddy,
Milam Smith and Rachel Stacy

Introduction by W. Geoffrey Black and Claire Reddy

To Amesbury MM,

[signature]

A project of QUIP
published jointly by

Quaker Press of Friends General Conference, USA,
and Quaker Books of Britain Yearly Meeting, UK.

US ISBN: 1-888-305-37-1

Design and composition by Trish Carn.
Cover photograph by Milam Smith.
Back cover photograph by Lucy Duncan.
Editorial board photo, page 5, by Bruce Hawkins.

Excerpt from "The Meeting" by John Greenleaf Whittier from
Selections from the Religious Poems of John Greenleaf Whittier, Tract
Association, Philadelphia, PA, 1999. Used by permission.

"Facing the Fear Factor" by Randy Burns and "Tough Times" by
Levi Fletcher are used with permission of Evangelical Friends
International Communications Commission, who sponsor and
produce the Publishers of Truth essay contest booklets.

For information about this publication contact:
Quakers Uniting in Publications
at quip@2quakers.net or go to www.quakers.org/quip

To order this publication in the United States contact:
QuakerBooks of FGC
 800 966-4556, bookstore@fgcquaker.org or order online from
www.QuakerBooks.org

To order this publication in Great Britain contact:
Quaker Bookshop, Friends House, Euston Road, London NW1 2BJ
Tel: 020 7663 1030, bookshop@quaker.org.uk,
www.quaker.org.uk/bookshop

Table of contents

Community

Spiritual journeys

Walking on Water

Epilogue:

Acknowledgements

Author biographies

This book and QUIP

What is QUIP and what is its work?

Whispers

I once heard a saying,
"Stop whispering, Start shouting!"
When I listened, it made sense.
But when I heard it,
And actually applied it,
I realized how untrue these words were.
With the shout or yell you are invading.
Giving no option rather than your voice.
You're yelling blindly into a night,
Never knowing what it is you're fighting.
Never knowing your enemy, ally, friend, or foe.
Or when they give in; when they give up.
But to whisper
Or to never speak at all
You have constant vigilance;
Never waning.
In silence you can hear your friends,
Hear your foes.
Yet prove to know the difference.
How better to make a stand
Than to *be* the stand
And not just talk about it.
And while we silently fight
For that heavenly cause,
We don't pass judgement.
And while we sit in our humble silence,
We get to not just listen,
But truly hear...
All of the beauty around us.
We can then experience everyone
And everything
For what they're worth
And not just what they react to.
We know the man before he lost everything.

We see the woman before she lost hope.
And save them.
They say, "If you can't beat them, join them."
No, it's "If you can't beat them, keep going."
So maybe some like to shout,
Others listen,
Some fight hate with hate...
I'll whisper my pleas of protest.
A yell dies out,
Whispers only get stronger.
And silence is deafening.

Aubrey Stanton, 13
Baltimore Yearly Meeting, USA

INTRODUCTION

If you had been walking on the beach near Twin Rocks, Oregon, on 23 April 2005, you might have noticed a small group of young people spread out on the sand tossing a Frisbee around. It was a damp, windy day, and the wind often caught the Frisbee and blew it far away down the beach, causing someone to run after it and bring it back; much laughter always ensued. In fact, this group seemed to laugh at everything – bad throws, fumbled catches; the futility of even trying to play Frisbee in this wind.

This group of young people is the editorial board for the book you now hold in your hands. The five of us had just arrived an hour or two before, and we hadn't yet begun our work as a board, but as we stood on the beach laughing, hair blowing in our faces, we were already building the working relationship that would be of tremendous value when we met the next day to determine the shape and content of this book.

That working relationship was based on a lot of things. A shared joy in being with other Quakers our own age; the excitement about the project we had come here to work on together; similar experiences growing up; similar (but not identical!) values and beliefs. We had differences in our families, our schooling, our meetings, our life goals; but we shared the common experience of trying to make sense of our religion, of seeking to answer the question, 'What does Quakerism mean to me, in my heart?'

The Young Friends whose writing makes up this book also share that experience. You will find many different voices in these pages: voices of certainty and voices of doubt, voices of fear and voices of hope, serious voices and voices of silliness. You will find liberal and evangelical voices, programmed and unprogrammed voices. Above all, you will find voices of faith. If there is one message we want this book to convey, it is that young Friends' voices may not be loud, but we do have things to say, and we are speaking. This book is not at all exhaustive; it doesn't include every possible experience and it is not a perfect, statistically representative sample of Quaker youth. However, we feel that it captures a broad, diverse range of experiences; we hope it will serve as a catalyst and an inspiration for more young Friends to tell their stories and make their voices heard, whether through writing, artwork, or simply through the way they live their lives. It is our hope that it will inspire a greater fellowship between young Friends and older, and a greater sense of community among young Friends.

When we sat down to sift through the submissions for this book – the day following that impromptu Frisbee game on the beach – something beautiful happened. We came into the process with very few preconceived notions, unsure what kind of book would come out of it, and as we worked together, the book seemed to take shape on its own, growing into something better than any of us could possibly have come up with through careful, methodical planning. Our decisions, some easy, some difficult, were tangibly spirit-led. We were not imposing our will on the book, but simply helping it grow toward what it was already becoming. As our meeting drew to a close – near three o'clock in the morning – most people would only have seen some messy piles of paper and a handful of tired people in that room. As we struggled to keep our eyes open, however, we could clearly feel that there was a book in the room with us. There was a lot of work still to be done, but the dry seed we had started out with – an idea, and some pieces of writing – had germinated into a small, tender, beautiful, growing thing. We cannot take any more responsibility for this book than a gardener can take for the miracle performed by sun, rain, soil and seed; but it was an honour to be present to observe that miracle, and help out as much as we could.

There was one thing we experienced, over and over again, as we read through the submissions. Certain pieces simply rang true, because they spoke of our own experiences. Whether you are young or old, Quaker or non-Quaker, we hope at some point in reading this book you will experience what we did; we hope you will hear your own voice speaking to you through another's words, or find yourself looking out on a familiar place through another's eyes. As you read, listen for those pieces that ring true as echoes of your own journey. There may be times when you find obvious similarities; a description of a gathering you also attended, or a quote from a song you also sing. Perhaps, though, you will find a shared experience in a much more subtle way, hidden behind layers of seemingly overwhelming differences, a similarity popping up in a place you didn't expect to find any. Open your heart to these experiences and the diversity among them; you may be surprised at what you find in unexpected places. As we learn to see ourselves reflected in others from the entire spectrum and age range of Friends, it becomes easier to understand the "other" in others; one small similarity in experience can help bridge a chasm of differences.

W. Geoffrey Black & Claire Reddy
for the editorial board

From left to right: Claire Reddy, Rachel Stacy, P. Zion Klos, W. Geoffrey Black & Milam Smith

Silence?

"What are you reading?" asked Polonius of Hamlet. In reply the feigning mad, witty Hamlet answered, "Words." He was reading words. That was all. Though Polonius took his answer in jest and accredited it to his madness, I wonder what we read now in the 21st century. Do we read words? Or do we just skip the words and get the gist of what is going on?

In a society littered with words and little appreciation for silence, can we even claim to read words? In this essay I find myself carelessly tossing words on the page. I write without pause, constantly hearing sounds and not thinking about the words I put down.

A period means a break, but is it a break, a silence, or just a convention we use to put closure to our thoughts? Where is the silence in our modern writing? We are so fast paced that a piece of writing needs to grab our attention from the get-go or we drop it. No lengthy Victorian novels relishing words for us. Then why do we litter our writing and speech with unnecessary words? Like, um... well, I don't know, simply because. Because we are trying to block the silence?

Take a minute. Breathe.

No, really. My writing is cluttered. My life is cluttered.

Escape the cluttered speech and writing we have become. Find the silence.

Erika Marie Richter, 17
New York Yearly Meeting, USA

In a culture obsessed with speed, it's hard to sit down and produce thoughtful, grounded spiritual writing. Yet that is what the Young Friends in this book have tried to do. We hope you will honour their work by reading it slowly. Take a minute. Find the silence. Read the words.

P. Zion Klos

WORSHIP

One of the most apparent differences among Friends is our style of worship. Despite our differences we are all worshiping the Divine within the manner of Friends, and participating in both the baptism and the communion of the Holy Spirit. "For just as the body is one and has many members, and all the members of the body, though many, are one body, so it is with Christ. For in the one Spirit we were all baptized into one body, and we were all made to drink of one Spirit." (I *Corinthians* 12:12-13)

Unprogrammed worship is where a community of Friends meets together with the Divine in a quiet or silent meeting where messages from the Divine can be heard, and members of the community can listen to the Divine messages and minister with them. Worship in this manner can result in messages that speak of the Divine as Christ, God or the Spirit. The core idea of unprogrammed worship is that without an intermediary to God such as a priest or a pastor, an individual can hear the words of the Divine in a continual revelation and minister to the community. The choice of basing this continual revelation within the Holy Scriptures varies among Friends.

Programmed worship consists not of an intermediary who interprets the word of the Divine to the people, but has a pastor or a minister who acts as a guide. The individual who serves as a pastor or minister is blessed with a talent for ministry both in the pastoral sense and in the preaching sense.

In many programmed services, there is a place for quiet or silent worship, where members of the community have the opportunity to minister or reflect on the sermon. In addition, song, choral selections and scriptural passages are extremely prevalent within programmed worship. The style and compilation of programmed worship varies among Friends, as does theological interpretation.

Rachel Stacy, 19
Baltimore Yearly Meeting, USA

I hear God singing within me

I always sit in the same spot during meeting for worship. Nestled in the corner of the cherry bench my father refinished, I sit quietly, my head turned slightly to the left, where two hundred year old moldings frame a twelve-paned window. Since I was a tiny baby, my family has occupied that bench. As I've grown older and my little sister also started attending meeting, I have fought for and won the corner seat by the window. The view I have seen outside of that window has changed only slightly over the past sixteen years. I have changed though, and as I grow, how I see the view outside the window has changed as well.

I'm five years old and it's springtime. A bluebird hops from branch to branch of the leafy oak outside the window. I squirm on the bench, wishing I, too, could be out in the gentle sunshine, hopping and skipping and yelling. The heavy silence in the meeting room pounds in my ears. Impatiently, I look at our First Day school teacher. She looks at me sternly, admonishing me to be still. It is not time to leave yet. I again turn my attention on the window. As I look at the bird more closely, I see a little nest filled with baby birds. I can no longer contain my excitement. I stand up, ready to proclaim to the silent meeting room the miracle of life outside the window, when the First Day school teacher, ascertaining my intention, hurriedly ushers me from the room.

It's the Sunday before Christmas, and I am eight years old. Greens hang on the window, giving off the fresh winter scent of pine and snow. My friend Gina and my sister Madeline sit on the bench next to me. The three of us have recently learned the sign language alphabet in First Day school, and we use our new knowledge to painstakingly spell out messages to one another. I eventually turn away in frustration, and study the bow tied around the evergreen on the window. Its intricate curls and gold trimming remind me of my own life, which has become more and more complex over the years. In school my math workbook is now filled with multiplication and my class is reading longer books with bigger words; I'm a big girl now, and I no longer have time to color and paste. I look past the ribbon to the outside where it is beginning to snow. I hope that there won't be school tomorrow. And since it is near Christmas, I say a little prayer for the well-being of my family and friends and the speedy arrival of the gifts I want. I don't know if God can hear me, but in the silence of the meeting room, I feel more listened to than anywhere else.

The summer sun pours in through the window and beats heavily on my thirteen-year-old head. I sit, my eyes closed, trying almost too hard to find God in the swirl of thoughts that throng my brain. Finally, I give up and open my eyes in exasperation. Resorting to my favorite meeting house pastime, I look out the window and begin to dream about my future life. Rather than the quiet simplicity of Quakerism my daydreams involve elaborate mansions and movie stars. While I watch the adults silently worshipping, I keep my mind busy, making plans for when I'm "grown up" and philosophizing about the nature of God. My Lutheran teachers have told me that God is in the Bible. My Quaker family tells me to look for God inside myself. I defy them both and look for God outside the window. The summer wind in the oak tree and the sound of cars on the nearby highway combine to create a siren song of reality. I don't need to find any God-force right now. First I have to find me.

I'm sixteen years old this autumn, and this is my first full-length meeting for worship. I do not try to think this time, and I do not try to plan anything. Instead I sit quietly, my eyes slightly closed, and allow my mind to slowly empty. Any thought that pops into my head meets a whisper of "thinking" and then dies away. Before I close my eyes completely, I glance out the window at the thin fall sunlight. I allow this light to fill me, washing away everything else, and then, with a silent thanks to the window, I sit waiting for God. I do not find a miracle, no bright lights or angels. Instead, I find a deep cleansing peace, and I realize that life is just that simple. Theology and religion aside, I find in the sunlight from the window a simple feeling of pleasure at being alive and being me, and for now, that is all I need.

When I open my eyes after thirty minutes of silent worship, I find that I cannot quite recapture the peace I had found. Perhaps next week I'll be able to last a little longer. For now I simply turn my head a little to the left and allow my thoughts to drift up and out. And for a moment I think I hear God singing within me as together we float up into the vaulting blue sky outside my window.

Lily Press, 16
New York Yearly Meeting, USA

The tingle of God

Sitting quietly,
Patiently,
Waiting for that tingle
Or prickling
I've heard so much about.
I can hear every sniffle and whisper...
It's breaking my concentration.
It's too loud to find God in here.
There's a song running through my head
And my toes are asleep.
Brayden's sucking his thumb
And Carrie's counting her fingers.
Don is asleep and starting to snore
And my Mom is shooting me looks.
It's OK, I'll practice at home before next week
So I can feel the tingle of God.

Taylor Stanton, 16
Baltimore Yearly Meeting, USA

I open my eyes

It is summertime; muggy air greets my senses. I walk to the bed of a babbling brook, water so clear, earthen pebbles resilient as wetness trickles on. Moss beneath my feet is poetry to the touch. Summer green paints the forest and I wait. I sit still for eternities; they tick by like seconds.

I dress in bright nature like when I was born, and feel free, as Adam might have. He sits behind a wide forest tree and when he speaks, harmonies fall, orchestral and blissful. He speaks a clear, deep music, but I understand and answer him the same. He speaks all languages but knows I prefer this universal tongue.

He tells with sadness of the human condition, but also with jubilance of those blessed souls who make him proud. When he speaks of them, peace rains soft drops on my cheek. He speaks of them with such passion; I believe they are his children. When he tells of their tales, he makes me wish I could see them. They sound so wonderful in his articulate tone. I hope we meet someday.

It is to him I come, bearing hardships and woe, and he who takes the weight from my shoulders. If I come to him in silence, he will follow suit, knowing mere presence can be therapeutic. If I come to him in tears, he will soothe the ache and end my sorrow. He is fleeting as a deer, coming only if there is a proper ambience. If I should become something other than myself, he will not appear to me. If I speak naught but lies of him, he will not be waiting for me when I come. If I deny him outright, however, condemning him for loss, anger, and grief, he will open his eyes, stay his cautious feet, and spread a fatherly smile across his face. He is there because of me.

I feel his warmth, a radiance. Sanctuary and forgiveness his skin exudes. He is close, so dearly close to me, that I can almost reach out and touch him. My hand moves toward his shoulder – and I open my eyes. Fluorescence lights him and brightens a white ceiling. The green carpet below is cast like a vast shadow. I was not dreaming in my meeting house chair. It was my Sunday morning salvation.

Daniel Murphy, 14
Baltimore Yearly Meeting, USA

Silence
Claire Reddy

Encircling silence

A circle of silence,
Life flowing around.
Hearts opened wide –
The meaning, out.

Noises subside
Endless chatter, stops.
The feeling pours round
Life's messages, clear.

Quiet music ringing,
Speech gone far away –
Creatures stop to listen to
The silent circle, singing.

Brianna Richardson, 17
North Pacific Yearly Meeting, USA

Silence

Stillness...
The cricket chirps – the owl flies
Listen to the quiet noises, of the world
All is silent, open, unrestrained.

I never heard them – talk, out loud
For they only spoke through silence
I listened close, and then I heard
Those silent, whispering voices.

Listen to those murmurs soft
That never come your way
Quiet now and listen to
That silence, whispering –

Brianna Richardson, 17
North Pacific Yearly Meeting, USA

Prayer

The meeting for worship seems to be a sphere of existence set apart from the vicissitudes and uncertainties of day-to-day living: a place where one can open one's mind to God, in prayer and in worship, and thus move closer to him, sense his presence, and absorb oneself in the silence and spiritual intensity of communal worship. This time alone with one's thoughts and yet simultaneously sharing the joy of God's presence in unity with other Friends is an integral part of the week; but the danger lies in feeling that the act of prayer stops when leaving the meeting house.

For me, prayer is an unceasing activity and lies in the constant and full-hearted devotion of oneself to God's will. Prayer comprises both the act of worship itself and the silent contemplation of community, self and God that that implies, and the actual carrying out of God's will during the week. Prayer is a communication with God, and implies therefore a reciprocal relationship. God, through the divine promptings of the Light within me, can show me in what direction his will lies, and I, in my limited way, can attempt to follow the path he has shown me.

Silent prayer starts but does not end with the meeting. Silent prayer continues throughout the week in a never-ceasing endeavour to move closer to and ultimately to achieve oneness with God. Through moments of silent contemplation and communication with the divine, with 'that of God' within me, a meaningful and loving relationship is achieved. A constant joyous offering of the spirit to his will and awareness of his consistent presence, guidance, and, primarily, love, cements the relationship. Silent prayer inspires fragmentary appreciation of God's beauty and of the strength his forgiveness and trust can offer. Silent prayer need not necessarily take the form of words, coherent thoughts or specific supplication, but is rather an immersion in the divine will through stillness and tranquility, in whatever way seems right: this is, after all, an individual connection. There is also a need to remember those in need through silent, loving, concentrated prayer, and to hold them thus in compassion.

Active prayer, like silent prayer, should be practiced unceasingly. In every appeal to the capacity for love and goodness that I see every day, suppressed perhaps but nonetheless there, in myself and in others, I am practicing active prayer. In sharing my witness with other seekers of the truth, while hearing their thoughts, I can move closer to them and God in a spirit of eagerness to discover new facets of God's beings and new ways in which to carry out his will. For this I am eternally grateful: that even though I have numberless flaws, even though I have committed numberless transgressions against his will, I can still be a vessel of truth and love if I open my mind to his way in prayer. Each sin of mine hurts God but also, paradoxically, brings me closer to realizing the truth as through them he reveals to me the unfathomable extent of his all-encompassing forgiveness and love.

Prayer, both silent and active, is the way through which we can see how to act as God's instruments on Earth. In seeking to describe prayer, the ultimate, miraculous communion with the unknown, ordinary language fails. It can only be inadequately spoken of as a more permanent expression and manifestation of devotion to God and to practicing his love by reaching out to and 'answering that of God in everyone'. Prayer, therefore, is not only a communication with God, but also a reaching out to other people and a communication with that of God within others. As a Quaker, I feel that prayer holds a special significance, in the emphasis on silent worship and hence silent prayer, and in that the high standard of integrity and morality involved in being a Quaker means that one is ceaselessly encouraged to practice prayerful activity. Prayer is an integral part of one's relationship with God and an essential element of the spiritual journey.

Charlotte Thomas, 15
Britain Yearly Meeting, England

In a Quaker Meeting

Silence. I wonder what time it is? What are they thinking?
If I knew, I could think the same thing, then maybe I
wouldn't be thinking about the time. Silence. Are they
asleep? I like her shoes – which reminds me, I have to find
a pair to go with those jeans.

Silence. Nobody ever tells you what to think in a meeting
for worship. Then again, nobody ever tells you what to
think in Friends. A potentially dangerous option, but then
again there's an ominous feeling that everyone will be
wearing at least one item of clothing from a charity shop by
next week. Pretty harmless potentials then.

So, what do you believe in? I must remember to take one of
those cards with me that explains a bit better than – it's
complicated. Anyway, it's not so much a belief as a trust,
not in any one else, or even in a book, but in those
occasional thoughts we get that suggest – yeah, there might
be something a bit special going on there. Does that make
sense? I don't think so, but I never have been any good at
explaining things.

Laura Herring
Britain Yearly Meeting, UK

Praise be to God!

When I sat down to write about my Christ-centered Quaker experience, I decided the best way to express myself was through the entry I made in my journal on the first day I stepped onto the Quaker path.

Journal entry 116, Sunday, April 25, 2004
Praise be to God! What an absolutely AMAZING day! Elly and I set off this morning on a quest for a spiritual home. We went to mass at 8AM, which left us feeling all right but by no means enlightened or full of You. Seemingly out of the blue, we decided to swing by the Quaker church near home and see if there was a service for us to attend.

When we got there we didn't know what time it was. We approached the door to investigate. As we were reading the schedule posted on the door and trying to figure out what was happening, the door opened and we were ushered in by a small, old lady with wiry silver hair. She asked, "Is there anything I can help you girls with?" I stupidly asked the time, and she responded, "About 9:30. You're just in time. There's a class over in the conference room that's just about to start, and I think you'd really enjoy it."

So over to the conference room we went, and we really did enjoy the class. They were reading and discussing the book of *Luke*; concepts of the old and new covenant; and how it all applies to us now. It was great. Everyone was so genuinely happy to have us there, every one was so friendly, so helpful, so warm, so eager for us to participate. It's as though we were drawn seamlessly into their community. Everyone was so alive, so vital, so inspired. Each one of them loves You, Lord, and we (yes! Elly too!) could see it, feel it. There was so much laughter mixed with so much insight. Oh, it was glorious.

After the meeting we went to the worship service, which was great. They have this quilting ministry where they make quilts for cancer/bone marrow-transplant patients. The idea is to provide a bit of warmth and a tangible example of God's arms wrapping around a patient via the quilt. Today was special, as a whole batch of quilts was ready to be sent off and part of the service was blessing the quilts. It was very touching. Also, a missionary family who's preparing to head for Russia in August spoke. It was nice to hear from them.

The Quakers do this silence thing that's really cool, where there's a period of time in the service where everyone just sits and listens to God. It was so refreshing. The best part of all is this: Elly wants to be in Your light! She checked the little box on the visitor card that said she's interested in becoming a Christian. It's not surprising. It seems like an environment where one can practically reach out and touch the fruits of the spirit, and nobody can leave without wanting to plant the seeds of those fruits. Both Elly and I want to join the church. Thank you, Lord! Thank you! The kind of joy today has filled me with cannot be quantified. It's a feeling of sheer joy, of coming closer to You, departing from the shadows of a cold, loveless world. I see your hand present in all of today's events, and the kind of excitement this instills in me is overwhelming.

"Incidentally, my name is Lois," said the old lady who opened the door to a new chapter in my life, a chapter I foresee as full of growth, friendship, fellowship and brotherly love.

Thank you for today! Thank you for the existence of North Seattle Friends Church, for the stark contrast you offered us between the old covenant practices and mentality of the Roman Catholic church and the overwhelmingly joyful new covenant practices and mentality of the Quaker church. And you could not have given us a more beautiful day for this to have happened. Beauty is everywhere in your creation.

Love,
Trillian

A year later:
This past year has been a year of growth, friendship, fellowship and brotherly love. Elly and I were welcomed into the church as members last month. Every day God teaches me new things and every Sunday I get a big hug from Lois.

Trillian Turner, 19
Northwest Yearly Meeting, USA

Self portrait

Trillian Turner

God Alone

The Quaker experience is one that I feel lucky to have taken part in, and it has been an important part of my week for as long as I can remember. It has meant a lot to me to be in this community, and to understand the beliefs of Friends from such an early age. The four testimonies seem entirely familiar, embodied in the gathering of our meeting itself. It seems that by now, the time of my thirteenth birthday, Quaker silence comes normally to me, it is so deeply embedded in the way that I think.

Likewise with other Quaker beliefs: I feel at home, and couldn't imagine being part of another religion at this point in my life. I have grown up with many mentors and great role models from our meeting, ones that have influenced me greatly. God, and Quaker meetings, will always bring to mind the image of the glorious sun, shining through our large ancient windows, casting beautiful silhouettes of autumn leaves on our round woven rug. This scene, beautiful and joyous as it is today, was surely observed in the nineteenth century when John Greenleaf Whittier wrote:

> And so, I find it well to come
> For deeper rest to this still room,
> For here the habit of the soul
> Feels less the outer world's control;
> The strength of mutual purpose pleads
> More earnestly our common needs
> And from the silence multiplied
> By these still forms on either side,
> The world that time and sense have known
> Falls off and leaves us God Alone.

Excerpted from "The Meeting" by John Greenleaf Whittier (1807 - 1892), lifelong member of Amesbury Monthly Meeting

Evan Lawrence McManamy, 13
New England Yearly Meeting, USA

Quaker silence

Quaker silence is special because when I am sitting in it, it gives me a real sense of serenity. I love to sit and listen to the sounds of my heart and the quietness that buzzes in my ears. Sometimes I can get lost in the silence. Normally I find that silence leads to a new and positive frame of mind. Or that Friends' movements or ministry help me to focus down. Non-Quaker friends have often told me that the idea of sitting in silence sounds daunting and scary. But there is something, and I have not yet decided what, that keeps me coming back.

Sometimes at meeting I feel nothing. All I can think about is coursework and the next party I'm going to. I used to worry about this and question whether my faith was strong enough to call myself a Quaker. Now I realise that in a way I am thankful for not being able to focus every time I worship. This makes the times when I am able to focus or 'lose myself' in the meeting very special.

Worship is a time to relax, to think, to focus. Often I really appreciate the sense of belonging, sense of support and unity that a silence can create. The stillness surrounding the silence is so powerful because although outwardly each person appears relaxed and motionless, within each person a sea of thoughts and stimulus from the meeting and the world may be flashing through each mind. Silence in meeting for worship is different to silence anywhere else, more gathered, and shared among the people in the room. The silence in meeting just brings a flooding of togetherness.

The silence for me has been most special when you hold with the other people in the meeting a strong emotional bond, that has been built up by experiences and is strengthened by sitting or lying still together, and listening to your own heart. Sharing silence and contemplation is powerful and supportive. A silence is 'gathered' when everyone has 'sunk into' the silence together.

I try to meditate and contemplate on my own, yet it is only when I share a silence that it becomes truly valuable. If I am sharing silence I cannot get up and leave, or move around or give up. In that way I am supported in being stiller and closer to God. Also I know I am supporting others, that if I was not there they might shuffle or move or get up and leave.

Silence – often I notice, listen and appreciate a lot more when in silence, observing the world and people around me. I use the silence to reflect on the day, the week, my life. I think of improvements that I want to make in my life. I consider people I should be nice to, and apologies I should make. The silence is at first a time for me, but as it progresses it moves out to the people around.

I use inner silence on my own when feeling low and needing strength to draw on. It can be shelter for me, but it is never escape. It is the opposite. I think that sitting quietly with yourself, whatever state or mood you are in, is a risk. It would be easier for me to keep on charging around with my daily life, not thinking or facing up to what I actually am at the moment. So when I do sit and look at myself I am happy that I have taken the risk and challenged myself, and I know as long as I keep doing this I will grow and make progress.

I feel comfortable and at home through Quaker silence, and automatically accepted. It gives me permission to leave behind my everyday busyness. The silence is special because of the special people you share with. It means total relaxation, love and honesty with myself. It means something words cannot describe.

Untraced author, Britain Yearly Meeting

From the silence

I sit in Silence for a little while
While I am thinking I begin to smile.
My mind goes drifting and dreaming without a care
From the fish in our oceans to birds in the air.

Then my thoughts come together good and clear,
And I know that a true leading is near.
My hands start to shake and my stomach to rumble.
I'm feeling my leading; I hope I won't stumble.

I get to my feet; I gather my thoughts.
My tongue feels all big and tied up in knots.
Then I grow calm and a new feeling arises,
Not of fear but the smallest of surprises.

Offering the message is so soothing,
The feeling of creating a new thing.
It isn't quite like preaching or giving a speech.
It's not standing to punish or even to teach.

It's just talking about what's being said
In your gut, in your heart and in your head.
The spirit of God is simply working through you,
And with God for a guide you know just what to do.

The message ends; I sit back in my seat.
Breathing so harshly, my heart skips a beat.
When my breathing has slowed, the centering begun,
I now feel that my message is finally done.

The silence returns all somber and deep,
And I'm sure someone out there is asleep.
But God finds a new heart to hear his soft teaching,
From the meeting arises a new person's preaching.
Everyone can hear the creak of her bones,
She brings a message in her calm old tones.
Its lovely to hear a new message be given,
As God reaches through to the body we live in.

Next First Day we get to do it again,
To listen for God to speak from within.

Daniel W. T. Hood, 16
North Carolina Yearly Meeting (FUM), USA

God can speak to each of us

My name is Hayo Daniella. I am an African Quaker. I have recently found out that there are about one hundred and forty thousand African Quakers, which is more than the United States, Canada and the United Kingdom combined. My father was born a Quaker, and my grandfather was one of the very first Quakers in central Africa. My home is in Bujumbura, the capital of Burundi. Burundi is one of the smallest countries in Africa, but it has a population of about six million.

I go to school in Uganda, which is two countries away from home. I take a bus to Uganda, and it takes two days to reach there. I started studying in Uganda when I was only thirteen. It was hard at first because I was homesick but eventually I got used to it. Right now I am fifteen years old in the third year of secondary school. I get to go home three times a year. I don't spend lots of days at home but I really like it. Burundi is a fine country even though it has been at war for my entire life, and you can't go a week without some shootings and rebels stealing things from people.

In Burundi, our church is known as *Eglise Evangelique des Amis* because French is the official language. My father is the pastor of the church. The church has seven choirs and they all sing on Sundays, it is always fabulous. I sing in a big choir named *Zaburi*, which means "psalms". It's a choir made of forty-five teens and adults. There are choirs for women, and children, and college students. Each choir is a spiritual group and has their own discipline. In *Zaburi*, girls put on scarves on their head to show respect to God. Everybody fasts at the same time whenever God tells us to do so. On Saturday we all spend the night praying and sometimes fasting. Being in a choir is about community and commitment.

Worship service always takes place for three hours, from nine until noon. It starts with everyone singing a song that everyone knows, and then the person leading on that Sunday comes up front and calls each choir to sing. After that it is a worship time where everyone sings. Then they pray for the pastor as he prepares himself to preach. The pastor often preaches for an hour. After that someone will put down a straw mat in the front of the church and the pastor will pray for the ill people and the people who have changed their lives and want to follow Christ. Two choirs will come again and sing when it's offering time. At last every one holds hands and they pray for the coming week and their way home. All Quakers in Burundi, Rwanda, Congo and Kenya worship in this way.

I do personally experience the presence of Christ. Usually when I am singing. And sometimes when I am praying or even occasionally during the preaching. I feel the presence in my body but it's not like any other feeling I ever have. I feel closer to God and close to other members of the choir. We often all feel the feeling at once but in different ways. I forget the rest of the world in that moment. It is just me and the choir and God.

It is good that we forget the world at these times. Often members of my choir lead hard lives. Some have been chased out of their house at night by war. But they come to church and sing. Singing heals us. I have recently learned that some Friends call this "being gathered", and that they experience it in the silence. It amazes me that you can have this without singing.

The first time that I really experienced God for myself came through prayer. I started praying on my own when I was nine years old. One day I prayed for protection and I really saw a response from God. Since then, prayer has become important in so many ways. I feel good and peaceful after talking to God. He always puts feelings in my heart to warn me of danger.

In Africa there are pastors and others who claim to be prophets and sometimes when you go and speak to them, they tell you crazy things and at other times good things that can help you. Often they will try and scare you with what will happen to you if you do not believe them. It is challenging to try and decide if they are telling you a truth from God, or something of their own mind. Praying for myself has helped me because I believe God can speak to each of us. I am learning to test what I hear from others by what Christ says to my very own heart. I also let God's Spirit open scripture to me, to test what I am told by others.

This spring I have been visiting in the United States attending a Quaker meeting called Freedom Friends Church. At first I thought it was strange because they sing a little, but then they sit in silence and it seemed to me like they were doing nothing, because no one was preaching. I wondered what you learn from sitting in silence. One thing that Freedom Friends has is a box with little cards in it that have questions, or advices, or scripture verses on them. So each Sunday I pick one. And that is what I ask Christ to teach me about during the silence. I like this – it is a way for God to speak to me in the silence.

I am learning a lot about Quakers. I am learning that we all listen to God—that we can all feel the presence of Christ, even without a pastor or a prophet. I am learning that we feel this presence in different ways. I am glad that I am a Quaker.

Hayo Daniella, 15
Burundi Yearly Meeting

Naxos from a distance

Milam Smith

TESTIMONIES

For Friends the most important consideration is not the right action in itself but a right inward state out of which right action will arise. Given the right inward state, right action is inevitable. Inward state and outward action are component parts of a single whole.

Howard Brinton, 1943

The testimonies exemplify the dynamic blend of belief and action – faith and practice – that is Quakerism. A belief not acted on withers up and becomes meaningless, but action (however well-intentioned) without a solid spiritual foundation is likely to be misdirected – futile at best, dangerous at worst.

Early Quakers were often persecuted for standing by their testimonies, especially, famously, those against "hat honor" and swearing oaths. Unlike those early Friends, today Friends are not usually confronted with such dramatic obstacles as jail and public whippings. Nonetheless, it is a constant struggle to live by our beliefs. Young Friends daily run up against the contradictions of trying to practice peace in a warlike world, practice equality in an unjust world, and make God a priority in a materialistic culture that places so many other things first.

In the course of our history, Friends have testified to many truths, and against many evils. There is no universal, standard list of just what the Quaker testimonies are. There is a great deal of variation between and within yearly meetings as to how much emphasis is placed on the testimonies. Still, many Friends would probably agree that we bear testimonies of simplicity, peace, integrity, and equality. Some would add community, but we have given that its own chapter. Some would use other words – harmony instead of peace, truth instead of integrity. Whatever the words, though, our lives bear witness to the same underlying truth: God speaks in everyone's heart, and when we listen, we find that we're called to live according to a radically different set of expectations from those that dominate our world.

W. Geoffrey Black, 18
Northern Yearly Meeting, USA

Tough times

(This essay originally appeared in the 2002 'Publishers of Truth' essay contest booklet published by Evangelical Friends International.)

I knew someone would have to stand up for what was right and I knew that person had to be me. I needed to take a stand in life, not just follow the crowd and do what everybody else wanted to do. That day I would become a leader not a follower. I would take a stand that day.

One day I was walking at school with all my friends. They were being very mean to somebody. I didn't know what to do so I went along with them and joined in, fearing they wouldn't like me if I wasn't like them. That same day I had football practice after school. They were picking on the same guy during football. The guy wasn't much of an athlete. He was no competition to them so they thought it would make them cooler to pick on him. They started pushing him and knocking him down. I felt really bad for the guy and I wanted to help him, but at the same time I wanted to still be friends with them. I went up to them and said, "If you don't stop picking on him I will not be your friend anymore." They stopped when I said that. They never did that again.

It felt really good to take a stand and help someone out. At first they thought I was a little weird but they got over it and we're all friends again. I thought it was pretty cool to take a stand and be a role model to someone else. After that day I learned that if you take a stand, they won't think you're weird, they will think you are cool. All you have to do is get over your fear and do it.

About a week after, I saw one of my friends do the same thing I did. It makes you tingle inside seeing that happen; it's awesome. I wish that would happen every day; every body would get along and more people would be friends. That would be the ultimate wish.

I think that God really helped me make it through it all. Making the right decision and taking a stand. If it weren't for him, I might not have made that decision. It helps me to know there really is a God out there. It has been a lot easier for me to make decisions now. Once you do it once, you get used to it and it's not hard anymore. Thank you, God!

Levi Fletcher, 12
Northwest Yearly Meeting, USA

Candles

I don't understand –
They're blowing out the candles!
Please, don't extinguish the Light –
Rekindle them instead.

How can you go around
Harming the inward flame
That doesn't ever burn –
Those candles don't do harm.

Light those broken candles
Make all glow tall and strong
Don't let any tumble out
Light the candles – light them all.

Brianna Richardson, 17
North Pacific Yearly Meeting, USA

Quakers: equality

I believe everyone on this earth has the right to express themselves. Quakers show that God is within everyone and that equality and freedom of expression is very important in everyday life. I think that sharing within worship and work helps to bring people together. It helps with issues effecting the lives of others and problems around us that build up inside us, unless we are able to let it go.

Being a Quaker and attending meeting for worship helps us to release what holds us down, and to bring to mind the people around us who include us as part of their everyday lives. Everyone at some time in their life is affected with that feeling that someone else is excluding and isolating them. Equality is where everyone is considered, everyone is fair and no one stands on a higher step then anybody else.

People in other countries (known as the so called third world) are considered different in some way and are led to believe they do not have a chance to be known for themselves or their opinions. Everyone deserves respect and a free path on the earth. Not letting everyone on the earth have the freedom to speak leads to friction, violence and war.

Exclusion is usually between communities of different races or groups. Exclusion is due to opinions and disagreements people have. This leads to violence and brings imbalance into the world, where some people have less, other people have more and some people are left out. People go through pain and torture due to the fact that they are different. Maybe because their skin is a different shade or they are part of another religion. Difference is not a reason for hostility, it is not a reason to kill or destroy, it is a chance to make others welcome, to accept all and to make the world a better place by sharing differences.

I think that if everyone worked to see within one another, we'd be able to drop our shields and barriers and be one whole. Some people cannot put themselves in others' shoes, so are not able to imagine or begin to describe the suffering of other people. Quakers help to see that the spiritual net between people can be released and that paths can be built over war zones and through dividing walls. We as Quakers – old and young – help to see the difference between every single living person on the earth. Therefore, we help others to see that as well by accepting and understanding. For we can not let be if we don't understand. It helps people to change to what is right if they understand the meaning of what they are doing. It also helps us to include and to accept, to look in the mirror and make a change with the person staring back at you.

In meeting for worship, sitting in silence and sharing both thoughts and presence gradually allows you to have a different perspective on life, whatever your age. In the Society of Friends, no one is ever alone and everyone is supportive and understanding. People are considered equals and all on the same earth, where there is one world and not three.

Sakinah Afiyah Hassan, 13
Britain Yearly Meeting

It's just a game

The controller rumbles as another sword bites another's
        flesh,
The Quaker's shouts of glee as the health bar ends,
And I sit and think of the paradox at hand,
Of pacifism channeled in violence,

I glance at my friends,
Quakers all,
Pressing A, Y, and Z,
Slashing here, chopping there,
Killing each other again,
And I mull the paradox at hand,
How my Quakers channel pacifism into violence,

And we know it's all a joke,
A bad joke, a deadly joke,
And we continue letting anger out,
With X, Y, and Z,

Our pacifism is our life,
But violence is the game we play,
And I pontificate on the paradox at hand,
Of pacifism channeled into violence

Owen Hayden, 14
New England Yearly Meeting, USA

Note: this poem refers to playing a video game.

Nonviolence

Through all his life he has stood as a bystander, watchfully taking note of an event, neither helping it along nor hindering its violent effect. It has been easy to stand by his testimony on nonviolence, and his other testimonies as well, when they were not put to the test. Now Tom wonders, will it really be easy to remain calm, remain in control, remain nonviolent with this fierce anger building? Can he suppress his impulse to join a militia, and give these soldiers what they deserve?

Soon Thomas' thoughts are bent not on hatred any longer, but on questioning. He realizes that violence in any form is wrong, and he takes note of its negative effects, even on a practiced Quaker like himself. He reminds himself that

> *Remaining nonviolent is not always to throw out your violent impulses, but instead to reflect upon their root, think about their consequences. Do not punish yourself for having them as much as not following them and carrying out their negative effect.*

With nonviolence on his mind, and pacifism in his heart, Thomas Hazard slips gently into a calm, dreamless slumber.

Evan Lawrence McManamy, 13
New England Yearly Meeting, USA

Note: Thomas Hazard, from southern Rhode Island, was nicknamed College Tom because he was one of the first people from his area to attend college. He was involved in efforts to prohibit the slave trade in Rhode Island in the late 18th century and was one of the founding fellows of Rhode Island College, later Brown University. He operated a general store in South Kingstown and employed handloom weavers to produce goods sold in the store. This imagined scene from his life is based on a real event.

Me – things I feel strongly about

I suppose the thing I feel most strongly about is the need for peace – peace within families, communities, countries and, of course, the world. Peace is a heading for many things though, as there cannot be peace if people continue to attack other cultures and religions and discriminate against them. There cannot be peace when leaders of countries are willing to go to war. In order to search for peace, we need to look at many different areas and we cannot strive for a peaceful world without feeling strongly about everything that is needed to create a peaceful world.

My hopes for the future:

I hope for a world where young children don't have to blow themselves up, fight for their country or work in terrible conditions for a small wage. I hope for a world where no one feels the need for terrorist attacks, world wars and nuclear bombs. I hope for a world where people from different countries can sit around eating chocolate rather than sorting out post-war agreements and sanctions. I hope for a world where jails are obsolete and soup kitchens unnecessary, where everyone has a home, food and every human right is upheld by everyone.

Jennifer Gulliver, 16
Britain Yearly Meeting

The richest 3%

I cannot get over just how privileged I am – in the richest three percent of the world's population. I have never had to worry about where my next meal is coming from. I have never had to live in a war zone fleeing for my life. I have never felt the despair of seeing a wealth of effort go in vain as a drought snatches away my vital harvest. I have never suffered from a disease which sickens me to the point of death. I have never felt grief on the scale of losing a family member. I have never been so hungry that my bones have pulled against my skin. And, I have no idea what it would be like to know that I was very unlikely to live beyond the age of thirty.

Alison Freeman, 17
Britain Yearly Meeting

Simplicity

I lie in a comfy bed reading a well worn book, relishing the free morning spread out before me. It is the weekend and I have no worries of work or people to see. As I read, an idea forms at first almost subconsciously but as it develops it engulfs almost every cell in my brain. It is perhaps triggered off by this one character I read about. He is a similar age to me but his circumstances are so far removed from mine as to be unimaginable. While only fictional, he evokes great sympathy in me. He must wake at four each morning to fetch water, tend to a few animals wandering around his yard and then prepare medicine for his AIDS-stricken mother. At six he walks five miles to the nearest town where he works in a sweatshop until eight that night. He must then walk back home before he can grab a few hours sleep until the next morning when it all starts again. And that's it, that's his life.

As I snuggle down into a yet more comfortable posture, various feelings mount in my chest. I know this story, or at least a few billion similar ones, to be commonplace. What comes to mind is the thought that if faced with this boy, how could I excuse myself, what reason could I give for the abject difference in our lifestyles and prospects. Try as I might, no such excuse or reason becomes apparent as it becomes increasingly obvious that there is none. There is only injustice and unfairness and I could never look this boy in the eye.

Comfortably snuggled as I now am, self-loathing and embarrassment have ruined any chance I may have had of relishing it. I can't see past such injustice and it fills me with despair and hopelessness. I must get myself out of this, to remain feeling like I do is unbearable. I force myself to think, perhaps I'm not as helpless or ineffectual as I feel. Perhaps there is something I can do to redress the imbalance.

Michael Wild, 17
Britain Yearly Meeting

Boating

Milam Smith

COMMUNITIES

Young Friends, when gathered together, often form the most incredible communities in short periods of time, an experience few know how to describe. Bound together by young energy and enthusiasm, young Friends find spiritual grounding among their peers in many contexts.

Communities of young Friends have the power to change lives for the better. We hope that you find the power of these communities in the words presented here by young Friends. There is a phenomenal amount of love to be felt.

Claire Reddy, 18
Piedmont Friends Fellowship and
North Carolina Yearly Meeting (C), USA

Shadows

When Young Friends meet together, we strive to foster a Friends community built on caring, trust, and love.

Excerpted from Baltimore Young Friends' Gathering Expectations

Imprints of people, outlined against a green field spotted with dirt. The grass fades from green to brown and back to green. In a zigzag fashion, the arms reach down away from the people's bodies, grasping their neighbors' hands. They blend, palms sweaty and sticking together. Their bodies stretch out, embracing the world. We are ready for everything. We are connected.

I was at a weekend retreat with my Quaker youth group, which consisted of teens from meetings along the East Coast of the United States. We were outside in a field that stretched out next to the meetinghouse. Lonely farmhouses and hills lay beyond the field, looking too distant. The outside world was forgotten as we danced around in the grass that tickled our bare toes. We lay down in a puddle of people. Arms and legs overlapped and intertwined. We were at home. Judgment was always left behind and we were free to let it all go.

The sun hung low in the sky, there were only a few hours of daylight left. Our worries dissipated into the brisk air that pressed against our skin as we laughed at ourselves because we knew it was too perfect. Off to the side, people played guitars together and harmonizing voices chimed in. The sound drifted to our ears, beckoning for our attention. Sometimes the guitars played familiar tunes; everyone turned their heads to sing. Our voices were raw, and our words were loud.

As we skipped and danced, our shadows followed along,

twisting and bending against the ground. Trees and faces blurred together as we twirled so fast that when we stopped, the ground kept spinning. Our shadows held no faces, no background. They saw no worried future. Although some stretched out further or wider than others, everyone looked the same in shadow form. There were no categories to place them in.

Together we collapsed on the ground, stood up and stretched our arms out toward the dimming sky. Bodies wrapped around each other and we bared grins of white teeth. Pure joy ran through our veins; we were free. Here I screamed out of pure bliss. When I talked, they listened, and everyone's voice seemed to contain so much passion. We talked politics over food that inevitably ended up whizzing through the air, covering our faces. Here we were all friends, we were all at peace.

Standing together looking out on the world, our hands melted together as our shadows grew long against reality. We all knew that after our short time together was over, we would go back home to a world with too much hatred, where our tears would be misunderstood, and everything we did would be judged. I knew that the only thing I could do is capture this energy, this spirit, and when I returned to the world, release it with hope. I knew that here, we were our own ideal. We all faced the sky and smiled at the irony of having this ideal and still believing it possible. We laughed because we knew that this was only a glance at a far better reality, and we laughed without shame because we had learned to enjoy it while it lasted. Here nothing mattered; here everything mattered. I captured the inexpressible the best way I knew how. I soaked in every word, every feeling, every shadow, trying to make it last forever.

Mica Whitney, 15
Baltimore Yearly Meeting, USA

Quaker camp

Quaker camp is a place where a group of Friends live basically in a community. We come to camp for different reasons; some people come for the simplicity, to see friends from other meetings, or for religious feelings.

On the religious side I feel camp has helped me. I had some beliefs about God, and if he exists? I wasn't sure if Quakers had set beliefs about God. If my beliefs were different would that make me a Quaker, or not a Quaker?

When at camp I thought about this and I plucked up the courage to ask a friend about what I thought and what she thought. I told my friend I don't believe in God at all and I don't believe he exists. I continued by saying if somebody put the argument across, "If God exists then how come disasters happen, e.g. going to war with Iraq? Surely God must influence it, good and evil." I told my friend that if God exists then he gave us the power of free will. We cause disasters because we chose to go to war with Iraq. These are man-made disasters. God doesn't influence them; therefore I don't believe God exists.

My friend replied, "What about cancer? People don't have the choice to have cancer? Why them? Why do bad things happen?"

I don't know the answer but maybe bad things happen to us to make us stronger and better people. If it wasn't for camp these thoughts wouldn't have entered my head. It just shows what I've learnt from camp – making me see things from different shades of light and not only from my point of view.

Elisabeth Grabowski, 14
Britain Yearly Meeting

YouthQuake

Lord prepare me
To be a sanctuary
Pure and holy
Tried and true
With thanksgiving
I'll be a living sanctuary for you.

Guitars thrum with melody as nearly two hundred teenagers sing along to the words displayed on the screen onstage. Some clap their hands, some stamp their feet, and when the right music comes along, many gather in the front of the room to dance their hearts out. The song fills the room and reaches out to the heavens above, a prayer sent by the youths, people from all over the United States of America, united in a common faith: Quakerism.

All of these young Friends are part of a six-day camp called YouthQuake, held in a glorious area of Estes Park, near the Rocky Mountains in Colorado. For almost a week we at YouthQuake sang, studied the Bible, met in groups, and hung out together. Speakers spoke about early Friends, how to practice the message of the Living Christ, and their own experience with miracles and God. We met many new people and forged new friendships, quickly bonding into different groups while still remaining open to new people. On New Year's, we held a talent show showcasing the many gifts of those gathered. People played music and sang, read poetry, and acted out small dramas, both comical and serious. We tackled tough issues, debating our different opinions on everything, from world events to the Bible. It is amazing how much diversity can be found within one religious group. But even in the same group, there can be dividing differences.

YouthQuake's mission statement is to "work to build a community based on love, respect, truth and understanding across the breadth of Friends." While I think this was worked toward, there were some differences among Friends that surprised me. "Programmed or unprogrammed?" was a common question around the campus. Programmed and unprogrammed Friends have different ways of worshiping, and this was apparent when we gathered for worship every morning and night. I know our program organizers tried very hard to accommodate everyone, and they did an admirable job, but it is impossible to please everyone. I heard some complaints voiced at my yearly meeting group that surprised me. They felt that unprogrammed Friends should be given more opportunities to experience programmed worship and have a bit more time for silent worship. Our opinions were heard, and, for the most part, answered, but this brought to my awareness just how different and diverse we are. It was interesting to see, as I did not even know about programmed worship until last year when I did a research project on Quakers. It was also interesting to see how many people had read the Bible all the way through and how many had not. I do not mean to put this in a negative light – far from that, I had a very spiritual and uplifting experience. But I do realize now how much work it takes to bring two different sides together.

YouthQuake has made me want to get involved, involved in peacemaking efforts and helping the world to become a better place. I have relearned my relationship with God, and realized that He is in everything and everywhere, and loves us over all. I could feel his overwhelming love for us as I sang and spoke with other young Friends like myself. He has created a truly amazing world full of joy and sorrow, love and hate, beauty and destruction, and hope. Now I hope that we all become more aware of how we are treating this planet and each other, and do something to save both.

Even now, the verse of a song lingers in my head, one which I'm sure will be familiar to most:

> *There's a light that was shining when the world began*
> *There's a light that is shining in each woman and man*
> *There's a light that is shining in the Turk and the Jew*
> *And a light that is shining, Friend, in me and in you.**

It is true – there is a light shining within each and every one of us. We need only to let it grow and shine out from within us, that we may spread the Light. Reach out to someone today (it doesn't matter who), do a kind thing, pray, sing, dance – spread your own Light.

Meg Nelson, 16
Illinois Yearly Meeting, USA

*From the song 'George Fox' excerpted from Worship in Song: a Friends' Hymnal, *1996, Quaker Press of FGC, #272.*

Quaker school

I have been at a Quaker school since the age of eleven and one of the things I have found to be most important is how Quakerism embraces and acknowledges differences, whether they be racial, or cultural or ones of gender and religion. Where there is less focus on similarities and an appreciation of individuality and difference, there is common ground for understanding which I think is part of what makes up the Quaker ethos and the integration of diversity at my school.

I love the idea of exploration through culture, through ethnicity, and moral values. I want to begin to identify what political ideologies shape modern society and challenge these subjective historical perceptions that have long dominated societies and instigated world conflicts and driven the notion of success and achievement through exploitation and wrong doing.

Sakinah Hassan, 13
Britain Yearly Meeting

Naxos city

Milam Smith

A healthy addiction

OK, before anyone says anything, I admit it: I am addicted to national Quaker gatherings. I take every possible opportunity to attend, sometimes at great cost, and there is always a period of withdrawal after each one ends. Coming from a place where the yearly meeting has no youth program, national gatherings are the only way for me to experience a greater community of young Friends, outside that of my monthly meeting. Fortunately, such an addiction is healthy; it has been through this addiction that I have become a more involved and spiritually developed Quaker. I highly suspect, though, that I am not alone in this particular addiction.

In my case, it began with a national, FGC-sponsored, high school gathering called Young Quakes, which I first attended in October of 2001. In the years leading up to this first gathering, I had been participating in my meeting's youth group events, but it was rare that I attended meeting for worship. Slowly, I had begun to fade away from Quakerism, as so many young Friends seem to do.

At this 2001 Young Quakes (YQ), I experienced a community of peers like no other.

We came together as a community quickly, and the love and trust I found in those few days among everyone was incredible. I am always at a loss for words when I try to describe such an experience; needless to say, I was hooked. Due to the events of the year, this particular YQ turned out to be quite a special one.

On Saturday of the gathering, a group of us were playing *duck duck goose* in a nearby field during our free time in the afternoon. We had just started to play when another young Friend from the conference came running down the road in tears and proclaimed the news: President George W. Bush just announced that the United States had officially begun bombing Afghanistan.

At this point in my life, I had not thought very much about war and how I felt about it. Having been raised Quaker, I naturally assumed that violence was wrong, but I had never been directly challenged with the issue; had I not been in such a community on that particular day, my reaction would probably not have been very strong. Regardless of anyone's personal reaction, our *duck duck goose* game turned immediately into a prayer circle. The community acted together as one without question or confusion. We sat outside in t-shirts in windy 40°(F) weather for an hour and a half, holding hands, some crying. When we finally moved the circle inside, we did so by marching arm and arm down the middle of the street. Some opted to get a black armband; I did, and I wore it for two years as a symbol of my pacifism and mourning for violence everywhere. The entire experience was very moving; the love, trust, and community response was like nothing I had ever imagined, and caused me to seriously think about my own pacifism and spirituality. I began attending meeting for worship more regularly, and have since attended all Young Quakes and FGC Gatherings possible.

One of the beautiful things about the high school program at FGC Gathering is the responsibility entrusted to the group of 150 young Friends to run their own program for the week, separate from the younger children and adults. Each year, six young Friends serve as clerks of the program to guide the community through the week-long gathering with a Nurture Committee, and also through two lengthy meetings for worship with attention to business.

The first meeting for worship with attention to business at FGC Gathering in 2002 (in Normal, Illinois) was the first time I had ever experienced any form of Quaker process. As my attention faded in and out, I remember looking up at the clerks and wondering how anyone would ever want to do such a thing; these meetings usually lasted at least 3 hours. I still had a lot of growing to do as a Quaker. At the 2003 Gathering (in Johnstown, Pennsylvania), I began to understand the importance of business meeting and how important it is to the trust and responsibility given to us, and strove to remain conscious and focused for both. Each year I understood and cherished more about Quakerism.

Another vital part of the high school program at FGC Gathering is what was once called Oversight Committee. At FGC Gathering 2004 it was renamed the Care and Nurture Committee (CANC) and it has since been renamed again. CANC is made up of volunteers from the high school community and meets once a day during Gathering to address concerns brought to it. It was at FGC Gathering in 2004 (in Amherst, Massachusetts) that I first felt a leading for Quaker process. I volunteered for CANC, and I found being involved in the community in such a manner an intense and wonderful experience. During the meetings for worship with attention to business that year, I not only remained conscious and attentive, but I felt led to participate and voice concerns. Through the week I had a growing leading to be one of the clerks of the program. I remember my anxiety as the Discernment Committee took its time discerning the next year's clerks; in an effort to find relief, I spent part of the evening convincing myself that there was no way I would be chosen for clerk, and that that was OK; those chosen are the ones discerned to be the best for the service to the community. When they finally finished and announced the names of the clerks and my name was called, it was one of the most thrilling moments of my life. Quaker process has become a very strong leading of mine.

My addiction to national gatherings persists as I continue to grow as a person and as a Friend. Though it is a struggle to remain spiritual between First Days and gatherings – finding the time, place, and focus to sit quietly for awhile is nearly impossible – I continue to try. With national gatherings as a jumping off point, Quakerism has become central to my way of being.

Claire Reddy, 18
Piedmont Friends Fellowship/
North Carolina Yearly Meeting (C), USA

SPIRITUAL JOURNEYS

We all travel the road of life. Some of us travel one path, while others take another. There is no one path to travel. Luckily, we are not the first ones to travel on a spiritual journey. We can see where others have traveled along the road. And to do this, a map is needed. What follows is that road map, not to be followed directly, but to show where others have traveled on their spiritual journeys. Perhaps we follow, or we take a road less traveled. But, wherever our roads may take us, the goal is to find ourselves and our spirituality at the end of the journey.

P. Zion Klos, 18
Northern Yearly Meeting, USA

A query

Do I set aside time for myself during the day?
Or do I wear myself out all around all day?
Do I know who I am? Do I care for my light?
Or are my stress levels rising beyond my control?

Can I simply listen to that radiant light,
        My inner light that yearns for rediscovery?
Am I sacrificing myself for the other things,
        the material pressures upon me all day?
Or will I take time to feed that flickering candle?

Will I care for the Light around me,
        and cause them all to glow more brightly?
Will I search for the hidden, and take out the darkness?
Can I, through sharing light, help us all glow stronger?

Brianna Richardson, 17
North Pacific Yearly Meeting, USA

Midnight glare

Milam Smith

My journey to faith

I opened the medicine cabinet. This is it I thought. *I wonder which one of these will kill me the fastest, how much will I have to take, what ingredient should I be looking for*? My eyes rested on my father's blood pressure medication. *Maybe this one*? I couldn't think of any of the other medicines that would be fatal. I picked up the little white bottle to look at the ingredients and immediately my hand put the bottle back. I was shaking; I closed the cabinet door and looked at myself in the mirror. I looked at myself for a long time. The hopelessness, the grayness within me dropped like a weight in my stomach. I did not know how I knew, but I did; it was not my time to die, not then. I ran back into my room, silent tears pouring out of me, physically and spiritually. I never told a soul about death, only God knew.

My world started the minute I gave life a second chance. When I put the bottle down and dedicated myself to living, I knew I had experienced something I could not explain. God had something in mind for me, and it was not my time to go, it was not my day to die.

I grew up in a Quaker household. Based on the east coast, liberal Quakerism provided a framework for me in which to find my faith. Left alone to work on my own spirituality in whichever way God wanted, the faith of my family was unknown to me. I knew that we were Quaker, and that we went to meeting every Sunday, but no one spoke about faith, no one spoke about God or Christ except in the colorful children's Bible book; many people spoke from the silence, but I did not hear God speaking to me through their words.

The power of life transforms. The darkest days of my life were days when life did not matter, and prayer was forgotten. There is no explanation why I came out of the darkness into the light the way I did when I was in eighth grade, but that event marked a beginning of the development of my spirituality. Now, five years later, I am listening to the voice of God call me into leadership and ministry, and I question what else God has in store for my life.

At first, after my transformation, I just talked to God. In this case, God told me that I had been chosen to live for a purpose, but I must work hard at improving and healing myself so that I could pass tests and become what I was meant to be. As the first couple of years passed, I was in constant dialogue with God wherever I went, singing in the rain and standing in the shower. But as the years started adding up, I started looking more into what I was "supposed to believe," this Quakerism, this Christianity. Instead of differences, I found similarities. Christ's teachings were what I had discovered for myself to be the truth, but Christianity brought those teachings a step closer.

Christianity, although not perfect, established a group of people who were not afraid to worship and a lifestyle which dedicated itself to service. Christianity was real because it consisted of the divine and the human, and brought them together with the intention of improving the world. Even with these foundations, I struggled greatly whether to consider myself a Christian or not. I could comfortably accept Quaker principles, even though they were based in Christianity, because the principles outlined a way of life which was not hurtful to others. I had read too many stories of people justifying violence with their Christian beliefs to comfortably accept Christianity as my own. At the same time, the similarities between what truth I had discovered in my own spirituality and Christianity were too numerous for 'me to not consider myself a Christian'.

I would like to say that I discovered Jesus, or an angel with a flaming sword came down from heaven and spoke to me, but my coming to terms with Christianity was a quiet journey to a questioning acceptance; a process of trusting God's leadings, even though I may be uncomfortable with them.

So as I have explored Christianity and accepted Christianity, I have struggled deeply along the way, with trusting God, listening to God, and speaking about God. A call to ministry has struck me with great discomfort but incredible truth. This call, this leading, frightens me with its power. In response to my fear of God's messages, sometimes I act in ways I know that are wrong so that I can convince myself that I am not worthy enough to listen to God. Fortunately God does not appeal to my logic. Instead God shows me blessing and love through other parts of my life. The hidden faith of my family and home community has revealed to me its support and religious intensity. My community here at Earlham College has encouraged me to listen and act with trust in God's leadings, leadings that are encouraging me to work with other Quakers around the world. God has empowered me to strive at great things and as a child of the light, I hope to work with others of God's children to listen and follow God's intention for this world.

Rachel Stacy, 19
Baltimore Yearly Meeting, USA

Just silence

Quakerism is pretty special to me. I first went to a Quaker meeting when I was about nine years old with a friend of mine who was a Quaker. I was soon struck by how different it was from other houses of worship. There wasn't anyone preaching their ideas to you. No one telling you you've sinned if you've done this or that. Just silence.

I had grown up going to an Episcopal church, but stopped about when I was 7. After awhile of going to meeting just with my friend, I started coming on my own. It gave me time to think through my thoughts or just to sit there, enjoying life.

I also went to a Quaker camp when I was 13. There, everyone was loved and accepted for who they were, unconditionally. Camp was a place where you could make friends, joke around, and just have fun. I loved it so much, I'm going back next summer for a whole month.

Lauren Hoy, 14
Baltimore Yearly Meeting, USA

God in nature

One major point in my religious and spiritual journey has been when I first discovered god in nature. Something you may notice is that I don't often capitalize god's name. This is where I am in my process of understanding god and who/what god is and the influence God has over my life. For a long time my religious and spiritual journey continued down the same path, then my beliefs have split. My journal officially began the time that I first found god.

For the summers of my middle school years, I went to Farm and Wilderness camps in Vermont. During my second summer, a bunch of us took a day and went out to a potential site for a new girl's camp. The day was dreary, wet, foggy, generally unappealing. The day was misty – it was still raining lightly as our group explored the heavily shrubbed area. Yet we were to spend all day out in this wilderness. After a while of exploring, we decided to take a break to listen to the trees. As I leaned into the tree, I could hear the rain pattering onto the leaves and the bark. I listened more and could feel the patterns of rain in my mind. No longer were these sounds solely the sounds of nature or rain, I recognized that it was god speaking to me. As our group gathered again, the mist lifted off the mountains around us, presenting us with the most beautiful view of what the future camp might have. As this scene passed through my mind, I realized that god was letting me know that this was the right spot for the new camp. Although I have lost track of the new camp's status, this experience has helped me feel closer to god and it helped me to consider what god or the concept of a higher being means to me.

To this day, that one afternoon sticks out in my mind as when I had my first realization of god, and the connection that there is something or some presence greater than I in this world.

Mary Crauderueff, 19
Philadelphia Yearly Meeting, USA

Claire Reddy

The Quaker Youth Pilgrimage

(this was first published in *Quaker monthly*)

For the past few years, I hadn't been very actively involved in Quakerism. I would attend youth events regularly but was barely seen at my local meeting. I still classed myself as a Quaker, until a friend, who had no link with Quakers but who attended an event with my family, asked me what made me more of a Quaker than he is. I thought about this a lot afterwards and became a bit anxious that I wasn't a religious person. So when I heard about the Quaker Youth Pilgrimage in January, it didn't take much convincing to make me apply.

My journey began in Birmingham. I was full of anticipation to start fulfilling the goals I had set myself in the months running up to this day. I liked the idea of getting out of my normal routine and allowing an opportunity for something new and exciting to happen. I wanted to influence and be influenced by others spiritually. Mainly I was curious. I wanted to discover a feeling of simple happiness and satisfaction. The goal I was most scared of failing was needing to prove to myself that my relationship with God existed. I felt that during this first week it was difficult to develop at all spiritually, which was frustrating at the time. Now I realise it was necessary, in order to get a firmer understanding of what I wanted to gain. It helped to make the effects of my experience more permanent. I had to get myself into the right frame of mind and so it wasn't until we arrived at Yealand that I felt I could start to actively explore my faith.

We climbed Pendle Hill, an extremely tiring, leg-aching walk, that I would love to do again! We held a meeting for worship at the top where I realised how comfortable and involved I felt with the group. I was, however, disappointed to find that I didn't feel the presence of God in the intense way that other pilgrims described. Again, I became worried about my suitability to Quakerism.

The next day was my favourite day of the whole Pilgrimage. We visited Firbank Fell, where George Fox preached. Something about the atmosphere made me feel very calm and I found it simple to concentrate on the silence of the worship we held. Afterwards, I felt really refreshed and we went leaping through bogs on the hillside, up to the highest peak in the powerful wind.

We visited Lancaster Jail, the Quaker Tapestry in Kendal and Swarthmoor Hall. We also experienced a rather 'different' meeting for worship, sitting in a graveyard next to a farm, and, let's just say, the sheep were very keen to minister and we all ended up in fits of laughter.

Barmoor, a Quaker hostel in North Yorkshire, was the most meaningful part of the month for me. It was relaxed with a lot of free time, but I chose to spend a fair amount of it on my own. I found myself actually interested in *Quaker faith and practice* (of Britain Yearly Meeting). I had never touched it before, so when asked to find my favourite passage to read I felt very lost. But flicking through it, there were so many enlightening ideas, and I eventually settled for reading passage 26.37, which I now read regularly.

Two of the leaders and one pilgrim were part of programmed meetings, and they spoke to us about the way they worshipped. Both leaders were pastors at different meetings. I had always been quite sceptical about meetings that weren't fully silent and having some members of the meeting being more important than others. It seemed to go against Quaker beliefs of equality, but the way they explained their roles made a lot of sense. They were seen in meeting to be only as important as the other members: they could not control or overrule others. They took it in turns with the other pastors to organise the programme, but there was always time made for some open worship. I was disappointed not to take part in a programmed meeting and was surprised to find so many of the Americans came from unprogrammed meetings, but although I think it would have been an interesting experience, I might find it difficult to centre down with only short silences. However, what I did prefer about programmed meetings was that members of a meeting could turn to pastors for help with problems in their life, or for guidance in ministry. They mentioned teaching children from an early age about ministry, which for me would have been very useful. I've always been afraid of ministering, not knowing if what I have to say is important and worrying that I'll express myself badly. I think I have found it difficult to understand the importance of ministry because as a child I never experienced more than 15 minutes at the end of meeting and so have only just become familiar with the development throughout an hour. This has made it hard to feel involved in the worship. I believe it is important that children have the confidence to allow God to speak through them and even a lot of adults have difficulty determining the right time to speak. Pastors are acknowledged as experienced ministers so I think it's great if they can share their knowledge.

We moved on to Holland to focus on the subject of persecution. On our first day we visited the Anne Frank House. It was quite strange and spooky imagining that this was the same place that we learnt about during school history lessons, and I think the realisation hit when I saw the famous bookcase. I got such a strong sense of the original atmosphere and closed myself off from the other pilgrims to be back there with Anne. I did, however, have to stop and think about all the other people in similar situations. I found a book with thousands of names of people that had been sent to concentration camps, and I wondered what had happened to them. I think it's important that we hear personal stories so we can begin to imagine the suffering, but should it always be the same one? Why shouldn't everyone else also be remembered?

The most challenging day was our trip to Camp Westerbork, a transition camp during the Second World War. I had expected some really dead, plain, murky area but this was fresh and full of life. It seemed such a brave idea to change it so dramatically. We held an excellent meeting because everything seemed so quiet and emotional. We looked over the sculpture made in remembrance. It was fascinating – bricks symbolised each person who had died in the concentration camps and each was a different size. I found it interesting and wondered why particular stones caught my attention.

By this point, I was absolutely exhausted, missing home, but not wanting to leave at the same time! The last few days were very sad, with everyone coming to terms with our journey almost being over. We talked a lot about how lucky we were to be there and thinking back I have no regrets about having gone. I know that spiritually I have changed a lot. Yet I don't remember how I used to be different.

Since I have been home I have been attending my local meeting more regularly. I do pick up my *Quaker faith and practice* every now and again if I'm feeling down and I've begun to tackle the Bible! I think I have a lot more patience than I used to, I use my time more effectively and I appreciate the people I'm around and try to put them before myself. As I'd hoped, I discovered my relationship with God while I was away and conquered my fear of ministering. I hope that all the other Pilgrims are as satisfied with their experience as I am. The Quaker Youth Pilgrimage was (and still is) incredibly important to me. It made a huge impact on my life and my attitudes, and I never want to forget the things I learnt from it.

Lucy Entwistle, 17
Britain Yearly Meeting

Talking with God

For me, being a Quaker isn't easy, by that I mean there are a lot of hard choices to be made, and you're left on your own to get in touch with God, which is good. This being left alone means that I can come to terms with God, and at anytime I need. There is no minister there to tell me how and when to talk to God, or even to talk to him or her so that they can speak to God on my behalf. There is a down side to this though. Without anyone telling you how to do any of this, it seems rather hard to get in touch with God. Thus I have come to the conclusion that there is no "right" way to speak with God, just do it the best you can, and God will understand.

Calvin Alvin Taylor III, 16
Baltimore Yearly Meeting, USA

I felt God

Well, I've been doing a lot of thinking. Meditating, more like it. Today in my first class, it came to me that what I should be doing is making origami cranes for Mumma. And now, after having made a hundred, I know why. It's partly for the cranes, partly for Mumma. But mostly, the folding allows me time to go inward.

My life has been amazingly uncomplicated until this year. This year, I have left home to live in China, a land foreign in every way. This year, the two worst things in the world have happened to me: my best friend died, and my beloved mother was diagnosed with cancer. Yet I am still here. I am strong. I am stronger.

This I realized: I have no control over things like this. No matter where I am, no matter what I do, there are some things that are out of my control. I have to believe that there's a reason. I know now that I believe in God, because I don't just think that this is a coincidence. I don't believe it's coincidence that these things happen while I'm so far away from home. I guess I believe that somehow, there is a reason for all this. Not a good one, maybe. I certainly don't believe that God meant for my friend to die, or for Mumma to get cancer. It's more a feeling that since these things happened, there is an outcome... and that outcome, that result, is God.

Maybe when people are faced with huge stuff like this, they either "get religion" or lose it, depending on where they started. For me, it's neither. I haven't "got religion." But I felt God while I was folding cranes.

I also had an epiphany of sorts about the concept of "holding in the Light." I always had this vague idea that it was praying, asking, "Please, let Mumma get better" (for example). As I was folding, I realized that I was truly

Spring

Milam Smith

holding Mumma, and my friend who died, in the Light. I started out by thinking, "Please, let Mumma be well and don't let anything else bad happen while I'm away!" Then I realized that I didn't want to say that. The events of this year have been horrible and full of grief, but they've made me think and feel and grow. Would I not want that? Well, I'd rather have my friend alive and Mumma perfectly healthy. But three months ago when my friend died, I wrote in my journal that I couldn't stand it if anything bad happened to Mumma. I wrote that specifically. Now it's happened, and I'm still here.

As for holding in the Light, it's not about praying. It's about saying, "Look here, God. This stuff is devastating. Right now, the world doesn't make sense. But I can't make it make sense. I wouldn't even know where to begin. So whatever needs to happen – that is what should happen." Holding in the Light is an act of complete surrender, completely letting go and just trusting. Just trusting.

I often refer to a poem given to me when I became a member of my monthly meeting. It is by Denise Levertov, entitled "The Avowal."

> As swimmers dare
> to lie face to the sky
> and water bears them,
> as hawks rest upon air
> and air sustains them,
> so I would learn to attain
> freefall and float
> into Creator Spirit's deep embrace,
> knowing no effort earns
> that all surrounding grace.

It would be glorious if we could forget religion and remember God. I have found God. Not Jesus, nor Yahweh nor Allah nor Buddha – none of these. Instead, God is what I choose to call sublime love and trust. God is found in the reasons. It is a positive creative force in the world.

(Note: I wrote this in December 2003. I'm happy to report that my mother is currently in perfect health, the diagnosis being a false alarm of sorts. At least it made me consider my beliefs, and I got some good inner reflections out of it!)

Cait Caulfield, 17
Alaska Yearly Meeting,
(currently in Shanghai)

There is a spirit

There is a spirit which I feel that delights to do no evil, nor to revenge any wrong, but delights to endure all things, in hope to enjoy its own in the end. Its hope is to outlive all wrath and contention, and to weary out all exaltation and cruelty, or whatever is of a nature contrary to itself. It sees to the end of all temptations. As it bears no evil in itself, so it conceives none in thoughts to any other. If it be betrayed, it bears it, for its ground and spring is the mercies and forgiveness of God. Its crown is meekness, its life is everlasting love unfeigned. It takes its kingdom with entreaty and not with contention, and keeps it by lowliness of mind. In God alone it can rejoice, though none else can regard it, or can own its life. It is conceived in sorrow and brought forth without any to pity it, nor doth it murmur at grief or oppression. It never rejoiceth but through sufferings: for with the world's joy it is murdered. I found it alone, being forsaken. I have fellowship therein with them who lived in dens and desolate places in the earth, who through death obtained this resurrection and eternal holy life.

James Nayler, 1660

These words were spoken by James Nayler (1616-1660), an early English Friend. In 1656, he rode into Bristol on a donkey, imitating the entrance of Jesus into Jerusalem. For this, he was arrested for blasphemy, tortured, and imprisoned for three years. A year after being released, while traveling home to Yorkshire, he was robbed. He was found in a field and taken to a friend's house, where he died. These words were spoken about two hours before his death. They became the inspiration for my first choral piece of music.

I first found these words in a hardcover, blue-bound Pendle Hill Pamphlet in the meeting library: *There is a Spirit: The*

Nayler Sonnets by Kenneth Boulding. I was looking for texts for a choral work I had been asked to write by the director of the Friends Music Camp in Barnesville, Ohio that I would be attending that summer. I took the pamphlet on a trip to Florida in February 2001. On the way home, I was stranded for nine hours in the Detroit airport, and ran out of reading material. I began to read *There is a Spirit* repeatedly, learning the flavor of the words. I found the sonnets too constraining in form, but I realized that even though the original testimony was prose, the words could be set to music very easily.

While sitting in a very uncomfortable chair in the Detroit airport, with annoying noises and eye-hurting lights all around me, I started to write down ideas. When I came home, I worked steadily on *There is a Spirit*. Composing music is a spiritual exercise for me. Starting a piece is much like being in meeting for worship, waiting for the spirit of inspiration to strike, and then working from it. Sometimes when I am working on a piece I lose track of time, and the music is the only important thing. This happened often during the writing of *There is a Spirit*. Even sitting in the noisy airport terminal, with angry people and loud sounds all around me, I could find silence in which to work. *I found it alone, being forsaken.* I found it alone, surrounded by thousands of people, in a crowded terminal.

I worked on *There is a Spirit* for several months, with the help of my composition teacher. I decided to write it for four-part choir *a capella* (without instrumental accompaniment) because in this case I felt that instruments would distract the ear instead of filling out the sound. It was by far the most musically complex work I had attempted until that time. I preferred working on *There is a Spirit* to eating and sleeping, so it was done on time.

I finished writing *There is a Spirit* in June, and I sent it to Friends Music Camp ahead of me. It proved too difficult for the camp choir, so it was sung by the staff at the final concert of the month-long camp. Nayler's words continue to have a great influence on my life and music. He has helped me become a more committed Friend, and to join the small but weighty group of Quaker composers.

Aliyah Shanti, 17
North Pacific Yearly Meeting, USA

Me

At the beginning of this school year, I was talking on the internet with a friend of mine from Maryland. I had met her at Friends General Conference' Gathering several years earlier and we had stayed very close. I was upset about school starting, being stressed out, gymnastics being time-consuming, and I felt ditched by my friends. I didn't know what to do. I was in a state of hysterics, close to tears, and exhausted to the bone. "Hilary, get a piece of paper, a pen, and take some deep breaths," she told me. I did as she said.

"Now, I want you to make a support circle."

"Deanna, I don't have time for this. I have to shower and do homework still – I JUST got home. I need to go to sleep. I just want to forget about this whole bad day. And you're the only person I can talk to about it and you want me to do get paper and a pen? How is this going to help?"

"No really, Hil," Deanna said. "This'll make you feel better. I promise."

"Fine," I replied. "What am I doing here?"

"You're going to write your name in the middle of that piece of paper and write the names of the people who care about you and support you around your own name."

"I don't have any names to write around my own," I replied, wanting to cry more than ever.

"Fine. You don't think I'm here for you? What about Kate or Christophe? They may live far away but they love you too. And I know things are tough between you and Kenzie, but are you going to stop being friends with her simply because of a little fight?" Deanna listed a few friends I had told her about, mutual friends of ours, and even relatives of mine who she knew through various Quaker functions. As I wrote names I remembered other people who I talked to about my days, good or bad. And I remembered people who I held in the Light when I was worried about them. "Maybe they do the same for me," I mused to myself.

When I was done making my "support circle," I took a good look at it. I thought about each one of the people in that circle and how I took care of them and they took care of me. I needed them and they needed me. They were my support. It was a comforting feeling.

For the past year I've been more involved with Quakers than I had been ever before. When I was in elementary school I would go to meeting for worship, not understanding what I was supposed to be doing during the silence. I would count how many people were wearing sneakers, or how many women to men there were. Sometimes I'd count how many pairs of eyes were open. It depended on the day.

When I got into junior high I pretty much stopped going to meeting for worship. I'd want to sleep over at a friend's house, or sleep in. Sometimes I had homework, sometimes I just wasn't in the mood for being bored. I stayed away from meeting for worship for close to two years, going to weekend-long retreats occasionally and liking them moderately. I didn't know everyone and felt lonely. Plus, I missed my friends from back home.

But, at the beginning of high school I changed. I realized that the people at school who I hung out with weren't interested in a lot of the same subjects as me. I wanted to talk about politics; they wanted to go to the mall. We were in two worlds. But not until December of last year did I realize that what I missed in depth from friends in my town

I could receive from young Friends – people who thought along the same lines as me. Here, I got to know people's souls. At school I met new people and gradually got to know who they were. First I would learn their names, who they were friends with, what classes they were taking, if they had family – the basics. With Quakers, I often don't know if someone has a brother or a sister because we're talking heart to heart first, not last.

Young Friends retreats are where I find myself. In a hectic world where there are deadlines, speeding cars, and cranky friends, Quakers help me regain my balance. I talk to young Friends almost every night, thanks to the internet and telephone. After a confusing day l come home and talk to young Friends who understand me on a deeper level than even my best friends do. Being close to Quakers enables me to explore all my beliefs at once. I don't know exactly what I think about God, the Light, silence, Jesus Christ, or any other religious talk. I know that I will figure it out on my own, however. And I know it won't be like other people's ideas about Quakerism, because Quakerism allows me, with help, to figure out what I believe.

Quakers also instill a confidence in myself that is hard to find. I know that, through it all, I will still have them there for me. The support circle I made is made up of mostly young Friends, and I know that no matter what, I will not be deserted by them. I can be myself and not worry that I'll be disliked or slighted for it. I buzzed my hair last year, and got more disgust from school than I could handle. My friends were there for me, but I could tell they were scared of the stereotyping that goes on at my school. At retreats, people told me that I was brave for trying something new, that they were happy that I was comfortable with myself. And I knew that it wasn't an act. I knew that they were there for me.

I may not see young Friends as often as I see people from my school, but I certainly think about them the same amount. When I start to miss them I'll call up this friend from Wisconsin, or that friend from Pennsylvania and even if we haven't talked for months we'll catch up right away. I know that they will always be there for me, good times and bad. And they know I feel the same way about them.

I don't know what I would do without young Friends. Sometimes I think about people at school who don't have friends outside of town. I feel bad for them. I wonder what their support circles look like.

I know mine is huge. And it'll just keep growing.

Anonymous
USA

My Quaker journey

I began to think about Quakerism when Ms. Melanie Douty taught it to us in 7th grade. I didn't think that I wanted to become a Quaker then, but I began to think more deeply about Quakerism. I think that I am more challenged with the Holy Silence of a Quaker meeting than all the ministry duties I have had growing up.

Melanie Douty's class really allowed me to gain a lot more knowledge about Quakerism and really motivated to become a Quaker. The class was able to help me understand some of the true values of Quakerism, and the history of great people who were Quakers.

Since I believe that there should be no more wars and no violence, I think that being a Quaker would help that seed to grow, since all Quakers believe in the peace testimony. I believe that I could gain advice and knowledge about resolving things in a peaceful manner.

I grew up in a peaceful household, so there was absolutely no violence. I never really understood why my mom said we couldn't play guns as a kid. As I got older though, my mom explained to me that people were actually getting hurt and dying from guns and weapons. She also told me that playing violent games was not a way to live a peaceful life, and that we should respect the life God has granted us. This is very important to me because I know that all problems should be talked about between the leaders and individuals. It should not end up in a war. I even attended a peace conference about our current situation with Iraq. It saddens me to know that families were being broken up and destroyed by this war. I truly and deeply believe that the US soldiers should not be in Iraq but in the United States with their families. I also believe that we should be having peace conferences with the leaders of Iraq, and any other country that has conflicts concerning our country. I most definitely do not believe in wars, so I would not be able to join the army or any other military branch. I could not do this because I could not hurt anyone. That is called being a conscientious objector. I truly believe that all our national leaders should be conscientious objectors.

I had a hard time at a charter school. Boys in my class made fun of me. They made fun of my bookbag, my hair, my braces, and anything else they could. It was hard to keep focus with bullies laughing at me because I was new and different. I recently read a quote by Carrie Ten Boom that said, "If God sends us on a stony path he provides us with strong shoes." I guess that I really was on a stony path with the shoes that God gave me. It was hard to keep a peaceful mind but for the most part I did. I was able to ignore the bullies and not pay attention to their cruel jokes. I would not want to have the attitude they had. I would not want to hurt anyone like they did me. I have learned that Quakers have an Alternatives to Violence Program (AVP), and I think it is very important to have peaceful families and peaceful lives.

My mom listens to a Christian radio station, and on it I heard a saying: "We are on the shoulders of giants." That phrase made me think of some Quaker "giants" who made the Quaker path so we could walk on it. Benjamin Lay, William Penn, George Fox, John Woolman, Lucretia Mott, and George Lakey are just a few Quaker "giants" who made Quaker worship possible today. I know that I may never change people's lives as they did, but I am ready to do what I need to do to help and make it better for all people.

My parents took me to visit a few meetings this summer after I told them I wanted to become a Quaker. Except for one, all of them were great. The one I feel most at home with is Frankford Friends. I chose Frankford Friends because it has been my school and home-away-from-home for five years and counting. I felt a sense of comfort and peacefulness in Frankford Friends. I'm not saying the other meetings weren't peaceful, but Frankford Friends had an unexplainable sense of love and comfort that I found nowhere else. I feel so relaxed in the Holy Silence and I really feel that I should share.

One of the best experiences I have had is with middle school Friends. I think it is really cool to be with kids my age who are Quakers. My mom says I am a great teenager, and it is fun to be with other teenagers who are great too. We talk about a lot of important issues like the death penalty and the Iraqi situation. We also do a lot of fun things, like playing games, having dances, and doing talent shows.

Canoeing is one of my other favourite sports. Our team is called Frankford Friends Peaceful Dragons. We get into dragonboats and race. Dragonboats hold twenty-two paddlers, a drummer, and a steersperson. Before the race I enjoyed talking about cooperation in First Day School. We race on the Schuylkill River with many other teams. We do this to raise money for the Fox Chase Cancer Center. I love our name because we took one of the most ferocious, violent beasts, and by putting a single word in front of it, we made it peaceful for a great cause.

I have been studying my *Faith and Practice* (of Philadelphia Yearly Meeting) on my Quaker journey. I read a passage which made me think of simplicity in my life. My mom told me that a pair of Nikes costs the same as three or four pairs of sneakers at Payless. I think that it is wrong to make Indonesian children work and work for so little money, when we could make the same sneakers here for just a few dollars more. From *Faith and Practice*, page 83, it says "Live and work in the plainness and simplicity of a true follower of Christ." I know that it is hard for me in my daily life to live as simply as possible. This is hard because there are always new luxuries out that are so convincing that I want to buy them. I know that I really need to focus on what I need and not just what I want.

I am very excited because although I am ending this essay, I am just beginning my Quaker journey.

Richard George, 13
Philadelphia Yearly Meeting, USA

Early stages of love

I love my two traditions, my faiths.

When I think of Judaism, I think of the fat knitted dreidls my aunt made for my brother and me, bulging with gold chocolate coins on Hannukah. I think of my nuclear family gathering around to light the menorah, our expectant faces, and the anticipation of nightfall.

I think of my Dad's relatives, radiating nervous energy and emotions, the intensity of their debates giving my mother headaches. I think of eating at their favorite greasy kosher diner. I think of the woman taking our orders. She has streaked temples and a skintight gray dress stretching across her ample hips and rolls and curves.

I think of all the rabbis I've ever known: the red-haired woman from New York who teaches and argues with equal passion, the transcendental blonde woman with a tambourine and a never-ending service, the young man who patiently answers my brother's questions about dinosaurs and aliens with directly relating passages from Jewish scripture.

When I think of Quakerism, I think of my mother first, the spiritual seeker she's been her whole life.

I think about being in a Friends meeting, everyone sitting in silence in a circle. The people are calm; their faces are devoid of desire or pain. They are like monks meditating on a winter mountain. When the Spirit moves them, they stand up to speak slowly of their spiritual thought or past experience, their voices warm, rolling, full. I think, amazed, "This is living wisdom." When Old Main's bells chime, we stand up, stretch out the stillness that has seeped into our skin, and join hands. We buzz with life as we make eye contact with everyone in the circle, hum in silent ebullience; we are tapped into ancient wells of peace.

I think of chilly mornings spent at a Quaker retreat, my bare feet traveling quickly across dewy grass, to find solace in the central lodge. I start my day with an organic plum, the juice tangy in my mouth. The Friends sitting next to me at the table have wakeful minds while I am still so sleepy.

Judaism and Quakerism give me so much. I take in their ideals, nourish myself on the traditions, the practices rich as buttery cake. I see my friend's soul wisping in her breath because my traditions give me beads of clarity, day by day. We are One in love.

Natasha Bullock-Rest, 17
South Central Yearly Meeting, USA

What Quakers mean to me

I haven't any idea what I believe religiously. I only know that I am still exploring. I also know that without Quakerism I would be a different person. I don't have any regrets but I know that Quakerism has altered the way I look on life for the better.

My previous friends think I'm in some sort of cult but I'll let them think what they like.

I think that open-mindedness is the only way to survive within a community of people with different backgrounds and beliefs and being an attender at meeting and listening to inspirational ministry has really helped me to reinforce all that I believe.

Catherine Playfair, 15
Britain Yearly Meeting

Young Quakers: talking about myself

Being brought up in the Church of England just didn't appeal to me. Countless times I was fidgeting and desiring to go home. My parents joked that when I was confirmed I could have free wine and food. This made me think – do I want to be bored in an old, sombre church, learning why we must do this and that, and be led into believing that certain things are good or bad and how we are going to hell if we do something bad?

As a Quaker meeting house is within walking distance from my home, our family decided to go there and see what it was like. That was seven years ago, and since then we have never looked back.

Being a Quaker has actively freed up my life, so that I can now think deeply about matters in the world and give my own opinions on them. Also it encourages me to be friendlier to people. I have made friends, too numerous to mention, because of this shaking hands with faces old and new after worship. It really does make a difference. Also, I can channel whatever I want into my thoughts – the silence allows me to do so. It is also an opportunity to speak in front of other Quakers during worship. What is so rewarding is that afterwards instead of just rushing home to watch football or do other things, people stay behind and have conversations about topics that were brought up in worship. I have been able to share my thoughts about the death of my grandparents. The atmosphere of togetherness at such times is wonderful. In the Church of England services I found this very difficult to achieve.

Lastly, although I play football and rugby, I do not retaliate or use innuendoes in an attempt to hurt someone. This restraint has benefited me far more than simply having a fight or verbally attacking somebody. I realise that the Quaker peace testimony has entered my life and is leading me in this.

Untraced author
Britain Yearly Meeting

Where I stand with Quakerism

I have been to Quaker meetings for as long as I can remember, because like most young Quakers I know, I was brought along by my parents. Though of course, when you're little Quakers as a religion doesn't really mean much to you, or at least it didn't to me. My main memories of my first meeting, in a little black and white building tucked away in a little Welsh village, are of climbing the amazing twisty tree, climbing out of the window of the kids' room to go and play hide and seek, because the door was the opposite side of the main room, and painting a huge rainforest mural on the wall of the kids' room. There were a lot of snakes in our rainforest because I could pretty much only paint snakes and flowers.

As I've grown up, I've started to think about what I actually believe, normally at two o'clock in the morning at some Quaker weekend, while sitting around drinking hot chocolate and marshmallows. The thing I love about Quakers and the reason I still go to meeting is that they don't try to force you to believe certain things. I've met so many different people who have completely different beliefs, but who are all Quakers and all welcomed for who they are.

I'm not sure this has helped me decide what I really believe. Basically I don't know what I do believe, so it can't have really. But it has definitely shaped who I am and my approach to life. Belonging to Quakers has taught me that people don't have to all be the same and that everyone has something to teach you. I have sometimes lapsed as a Quaker, if you take it as defined by attending meeting. But Quakers have always been part of who I am, probably the best part.

Dot Greaves, 17
Britain Yearly Meeting

The schism chart

It is strange to think that a single piece of paper has had such a large influence on my spiritual development; but when I look back, I am quite confident that without the schism chart, I would not be who I am today.

I first remember seeing the chart around the time I was twelve. It had lived at our meeting house for years, inconspicuously rolled up in a corner, but that day someone spread it out on the floor to look at, and it instantly captivated me. I sat there and pored over it for at least half an hour, fascinated, even though it was a workday and I should have been helping clean the meeting room or take down the storm windows.

It was $3 \frac{1}{2}$ feet tall, $2 \frac{1}{2}$ feet wide, and printed in brown ink. Across the top it was labeled "The Society of Friends in North America, 1661–1989," and beneath that was a tangled, confusing mass of diverging and rejoining lines, making roughly the shape of a tree. Around and between the lines, in every available space, were notes, explanations, statistics, and comments.

Each line was labeled with the name of a yearly meeting. At the bottom of the page, in the 1600s, there were just a handful of lines; as they made their way up the page, they branched, and branched, and branched again. Some lines wandered off to the side and fizzled out into nothing; others formed spontaneously partway up the page, unconnected to anything before. Sometimes when a line split in two, there was a little bulge with an X in it. That meant there had been a schism; if there was no X, it had been a peaceful separation.

It was an astonishing, overwhelming thing to look at. It was full of words I had never heard before: Wilburite, Gurneyite, Hicksite, Beanite, Otisite, Updegraffite, Keithian, just to name a few. The notes were brief and terse, but they hinted tantalisingly at layers of complexity I had never suspected lurked beneath the surface of my quiet, peaceful religion.

A whole new world opened up for me that day. I think I had heard it vaguely mentioned, before this, that there were Quakers somewhere who called their meetings churches, and had pastors who stood up and gave sermons instead of simply worshiping in silence. But seeing it on the chart – seeing that Friends General Conference, which I had assumed included every yearly meeting in the country, was just one little cluster on one side of this very large piece of paper – gave the diversity of Friends a reality it had not had before in my mind. I had always thought of Quakerism as a small, comfortable family of like-minded people; but now, suddenly, it was something much bigger and more complicated, and I was full of questions about it.

That started me on a quest to learn more about Quakerism. Our house had always been full of Quaker books; now, for the first time, I began reading them. Here I found smaller, simpler charts, stripped down to a few lines: Hicksites, Gurneyites, Wilburites. I learned new acronyms – FUM (Friends United Meeting), EFI (Evangelical Friends International) – to add to the alphabet soup of Quakerism already stored in my head. And I learned the stories that went along with some of those little X's on the chart.

They were sad stories. Stories of communities torn apart because Friends – on all sides – were too impatient to look for truth in one another. Every time I looked at the chart after that, all those X's, all those marks of strife and disagreement, made me angry and sad and confused. I couldn't understand why Quakers, who have been witnesses for peace in the world for 350 years, should have so much conflict and division in our own history. I wanted to single-handedly bring about healing and reconciliation everywhere there had ever been a split among Friends. I knew that I couldn't, but it is still what I wanted.

At some point I learned that there was an organisation – Friends World Committee for Consultation – that included representation and participation from every branch of Quakerism. It gave me hope to know such an organisation existed, and when their newsletter arrived in the mail every few months, I read it eagerly. Like the schism chart, it helped open my eyes to the diversity of Quakerism, but raised as many questions as it answered.

Over the course of several years, though, by picking up little scraps of information from lots of different sources, I memorised enough names and dates and amusing anecdotes to become the family authority on Quaker schisms. I even named my chickens after them – Hicks, Orthodox, Gurney, Wilbur, and Bean. But for all the facts I knew, I could clearly feel that something was missing. Eventually I realised that I wasn't going to find that missing piece in books or newsletters. I wanted experiences. I wanted personal connections. I didn't want the "other" Quakers to be simply lines on a chart to me anymore. I wanted to know them as people.

When I was sixteen, I made a choice. I decided to overcome my fear of the unknown, and go out and experience the diversity of Friends firsthand. This decision became clear in my mind over several months, but the first time I officially acted on it was in January, 2004, when I put my forms in the mail to apply for the Quaker Youth Pilgrimage the next summer.

I did go on the pilgrimage, and it was a wonderful experience; but when I look back over the steps I have taken since I set out to explore Quakerism, there is another step that stands out more for me. Not because it was big, but because it was small, and tentative, and undertaken with great trepidation.

In March 2004, before I knew if I was accepted for the Pilgrimage or not, I attended a small teen retreat in Indiana. It was meant to bring together teens from all branches of Quakerism in the midwest, but I ended up being the only teen there from an FGC-affiliated yearly meeting. It was the first time I had met any programmed Quakers face to face, so I was rather shy, and I think the other young Friends there weren't quite sure what to make of me. I had taken the bus all the way from Wisconsin (about 12 hours) to be with a group of people I had never met before in my life, all from Indiana; and I think it was that act of peculiar dedication, more than the fact that I was from an unprogrammed meeting, that made me seem strange in their eyes. I spent the weekend watching, and listening, and not saying much. On Sunday morning I attended my first ever programmed meeting, but had to leave to catch my bus home just before the sermon started. I learned a lot, but I came home still full of questions.

I look back on that weekend now and smile, remembering how fearful and uncomfortable I was. It was an awkward, difficult first step on a journey that has grown more beautiful with each step since. That first step has led me to some of the richest moments of my spiritual life. As a result of it, my experience of Quakerism is broader, deeper, and more varied. I have still experienced only a tiny fraction of the full range of Quakerism, but even that little bit has made a huge difference in my life.

A few weeks ago, I sat and worshipped with about a hundred Friends from a large evangelical Friends church in Oregon. I had no idea what to expect when I walked in. I only knew one person in the room; the songs they sang were all unfamiliar to me; the form of worship was not the one I am used to. Yet the spirit I felt in that room – the love, the trust, the spirit of seeking together as a community – was the same spirit I feel in my own small, unprogrammed meeting. It brought me great joy to be there, lifting my voice along with others in those unfamiliar songs, and knowing that although this was not my home, I was welcome here.

Each time I step outside my own branch, I learn more, not just about Quakerism, but about myself. I gain more self-confidence, I become more comfortable talking to those with different beliefs, and I am filled, every time, with a renewed sense of gratitude that I am a Quaker. I will always come home to my own branch of Quakerism; I will always come home to silent worship; but I am glad to know that I can venture out into the wider Society of Friends and be greeted in the spirit of love.

I still hope for healing of our broken, fragmented society. But instead of hoping our disagreements will all go away someday, as I did when I first learned about our history of schisms, now I hope we'll learn how to learn from those disagreements. I have learned that if we are willing to talk about them, and listen to each other, our differences can be a strength as well as a weakness; and if we enter every experience with an open heart, there is as much joy in the unfamiliar as in what we have grown up with.

This August, I will represent my yearly meeting at the 2005 World Gathering of Young Friends, in England. This event will bring together about 300 young adult Friends, from all over the world and from every branch of Quakerism. Nothing like it has happened since 1985. I look forward to this gathering with excitement and trepidation, and the expectation that it will be one of the most important things

I've ever done. I have great hopes for the effect it will have on Quakerism, and I feel honoured that I will be a part of it.

My expectations have changed, though, since last fall when I applied to go. Then, I saw it as a way to finally fulfill my desire to build bridges among Friends. I realise now, that desire will never be completely fulfilled. It doesn't want to be fulfilled; it just wants to be followed. And as long as there are more Quakers in the world that I haven't met yet, it will always be there, leading me on in new directions that I can only imagine right now.

I might never have woken up to that desire at all, though, if one big, dusty piece of paper hadn't sparked my interest and curiosity one warm Sunday afternoon a few years ago. A dusty piece of paper with a complicated, powerful picture on it. Truly, God works in mysterious ways.

W. Geoffrey Black, 17
Northern Yearly Meeting, USA

Note: What I call "the schism chart" is *The Society of Friends in North America*, by Geoffrey D. Kaiser (with help from Bruce G. Grimes); fourteenth revised edition, 1989.

WALKING ON WATER

In the Biblical scriptures, there is a well-known story of Jesus walking on water, but within the Gospel of Matthew, Peter plays an important part. After seeing Jesus out on the sea and recognizing him, Peter asks Jesus to command him to walk on water too.

> Peter answered him, "Lord if it is you, command me to come to you on the water." [Jesus said] "Come." So Peter got out of the boat, started walking on water and came toward Jesus."
> (Matthew 14: 28-29)

When Peter got out onto the water, he noticed the wind and the greatness around him and became frightened. When he became frightened, he started to sink. Jesus reached out his hand and pulled him up. "You of little faith, why did you doubt?" Jesus responded to Peter's actions.

Historically younger members of the Religious Society of Friends "walked on water," or in other words, they did what everyone else said was impossible. Even today to live your life according to the principles and core beliefs of Quakerism rebels against the norms of mass media driven culture. As we share how we have come to our beliefs, how we practice them in worship, and what those beliefs may be, encouragement is needed to apply those beliefs to everyday life. To follow in the footsteps of our history of Friends, who defied society and tried to create the Kingdom of Christ on earth, is to walk out onto the water, and not be afraid.

Rachel Stacy, 18
Baltimore Yearly Meeting, USA

Facing the fear factor

(This essay originally appeared in the 2003 'Publishers of Truth' essay contest booklet published by Evangelical Friends International)

About two years ago, Tropical Storm Allison dumped over 40 inches of rain in Houston, Texas, over a period of five days. Twenty-seven inches of this rain fell in six hours. In the middle of the night my house flooded and my family and I had to flee. We tried to escape in my father's truck, but it couldn't cross the water. To escape the rising waters we had to wade through water higher than my head. To keep me from drowning my strong dad carried me across his broad shoulders in a fireman's carry.

I was afraid for myself; I was afraid for my family. The flood waters were full of snakes. It was dark and we couldn't see them. We couldn't see the ground beneath the water. My brother couldn't see the open manhole and he fell into it. Richie was bigger than my sister Rachel and almost as big as my mom. Because my dad was carrying me, he couldn't help my mom haul my brother out of the hole. Mom was screaming and praying. My brother was thrashing and sputtering. Rachel and my mom finally were able to catch my brother and haul him out. I was praying fervently, furiously, and fast that my dad wouldn't slip and drop me.

God sent a man bigger than my tall dad to help my mom, my brother, and my sister. This man had a flashlight to illuminate the dangers and he led us to safety in his home.

Since that time I have thought about that night often. God is like the man with the flashlight who helped us. God shows us the way to safety and he shines His light on things that we should be afraid of. God is like my dad and he carries us when we are too little to fend for ourselves. Today I look for God's light in my life to guide me and I allow God to carry me through the high waters.

Randy Burns, 12
Mid America Yearly Meeting

I hear the voice of God so clearly in the silence

I am a twenty-year-old Friend living in the eastern United States of America. I first came to Quakerism in my late teens during a serious illness which led me to believe that I was going to die. I had been raised in a Freewill Baptist community where I was placed in the path of hatred, exclusiveness, and other abuses from people who claimed to be Christians.

Therefore, even though I thought I was dying and I knew that I needed Christ in my life, I still equated Christ with those people who had hurt me in his name. I had let a few bitter, misinformed people define Jesus Christ and turn me away from him in the process. It was a difficult situation in which to be. If I suddenly died, I might or might not go to hell, but accepting such a hateful Jesus into my life was too difficult. I had heard of George Fox and other well known Quakers such as William Penn in my history classes at school, and I knew the Quakers to be more liberal (in a good way) than most other Christian groups. So one night during a very dark period in my life, I poured my heart out to a group of Friends on the internet. I was not sure what I was looking for, but I knew I needed some kind of answers. I was made to feel welcome, so I hung around while seriously beginning to read the Bible, cautiously, for the first time in my life.

Staying up all night long, flooding my couch with tears, being worn out from groaning (*Psalm* 6, NIV), all these things resonated deep inside of me because I was experiencing them in my daily life. While I knew my illness was not a punishment from God, I also knew that like all of humanity I was in a fallen state. I was a sinner with a capital S. I had to fully admit that to myself, then tell it to Jesus. I desperately needed Christ in my life, but not a hateful Christ who was full of judgment and condemnation, not the only Christ I had ever really been shown.

With the help of my online Quaker friends, I searched for a nearby meeting. Unfortunately, there were none anywhere near me. Since I do not have a car, I decided to write a letter to the closest meeting, to see if anybody lived near me and could give me a ride, and I received a reply in a few days. Unfortunately, nobody lived anywhere close and it was at least a three hour drive both ways, so for the time being it was impossible for me to attend meeting. However, they sent me various Quaker books, pamphlets, tracts, emails, magazines, personal letters, and notes. In this way I was spiritually nurtured and tended to by the meeting. I felt, and still feel, as much a part of the meeting as any spiritual community I've ever belonged to, even though I live so far away. I consider myself convinced, and I hold my own "one-person meetings" on First Days, where I am the only (human) attender. I hear the voice of God so clearly in the silence, and I feel the touch of Christ. It has become a treasured part of my relationship with Jesus when I can wind down and simply allow him to inhabit my thoughts and speak to me. I am constantly reading works by many great Quaker thinkers such as Margaret Fell, James Nayler, and John Woolman as well as more contemporary traditional Friends and finding myself in agreement with their views on Christ and spirituality. In the fall of 2005 I plan to move nearer to a "proper" meeting, which I will attend faithfully.

Through a living, breathing, relationship with Christ Jesus, the one and only son of God, I have found the security and peace that at one point I did not even know I needed. I have come to terms with my illness, and it is now under control with medication and therapy. Although I am not going to die from my illness, by having such a solid living relationship with Christ, I am prepared to die at any second.

Through Jesus Christ's teachings in the Gospels (Matthew, Mark, Luke, and John), I have come to an understanding of Christian simplicity, extreme brotherly love, and absolute equality among persons. One thing that concerns me is that so many Friends my age have never even read the four Gospels, much less the whole Bible. They have largely given Christ up for a form of humanistic universalism. Through my own personal relationship with Jesus Christ I have come to understand the heavy importance of personal prayer, repentance, nonviolence, and simple kindness. I have learned that nobody can define Jesus other than Jesus Christ himself. And he is not intrusive. We have to ask him to come to us, to nurture us, and to speak to us. We have to acknowledge that we are fallen beings and that we are in need of spiritual help.

I have personally experienced that Jesus wants us to come to him, whether through Quakerism or another denomination or even all on our own, but we have to make that first step. That's why it's called "free will." We have to read the Bible, we have to actually pray, and as Friends we have to know more about our Christian history. Nobody can make us choose to give our lives over to Christ, but when we choose to, we are granted unimaginable insights, peace, love, and freedom that would not have been possible otherwise.

Anonymous, 20
USA

Finding my roots

Is it my faith that drives me to be who I am, to do what I do? Blindly I follow the path that has been placed before me in my faith. I am trying to break through, to stomp through the wilderness and create my own path, without the aid of those around me. Until I realize I cannot beat my own path without bringing everyone else with me, as their faiths drive them, and in turn help to drive me to find my faith. I don't know where I am going, I am only building on who I am today, on who I was yesterday, and who I hope to become. I am trying to find my roots that I may grow tall, both inwardly and outwardly, to make the most of who I am and to fulfill my tasks set before me in this world.

Mary Crauderueff, 19
Philadelphia Yearly Meeting, USA

The importance of friendship between adult and young Friends

As young Friends move through high school and enter the adult world, I've noticed and experienced a tension present between young Friends and adult Friends, preventing healthy and important dialogue.

Personally, as a young Friend in Durham Friends Meeting, I've found that I know only certain adults – ones with whom I have interacted more specifically over the years as I have grown up. Often these are parents of other young Friends in the meeting or people who have been involved in youth group events. What's missing is the connection to the rest of the adults in my meeting; I've been attending Durham Friends Meeting since I was born and I feel like most members of the meeting have no idea who I am. In addition to that, I've not known how to communicate my involvement in various wider Quaker communities, nor have I known how to talk about all the Quaker books I have been reading over the last few months, all of which have been very integral in my spiritual development. Even Friends in Durham Friends Meeting, with whom I do converse sometimes after meeting, do not know of all these things with which I am involved.

I stopped attending First Day school in January of my junior year in high school and began attending the full hour of worship. I spoke to the two youth leaders about it briefly so they would understand, and then there was no further response - no one seemed to notice! Looking back on this, I feel that my meeting and other meetings need to be more involved in such a transition for all young Friends. It's not enough for just those adults directly involved in the youth group or First Day school. Everyone should be more aware and attentive of the young Friends in meeting and their involvement in Quaker communities outside of meeting. Young Friends are just as much a part of the meeting community as adult Friends; this is something I feel both adults and young Friends often seem to forget.

An important part of a strong community is the sense of familiarity and friendliness among everyone within that community. I feel there should be present F/friendships, or spiritual friendships, among Friends – young and old – in a meeting community. In recent experiences I have heard the word "mentor" spoken of in many ways. Many young Friends crave a Quaker or spiritual mentor, while some adult Friends are uneasy with the term, feeling they might not be "good" at mentoring. In some F/friendships, an adult Friend could become a mentor to the young Friend. I believe a mentor is someone who, after establishing a F/friendship, finds that he or she has more experience than the other, and then finds ways to nurture and nourish the younger or less experienced spirit. It is important to note that mentorship does not necessarily need to happen for a healthy relationship to develop. Either way, in F/friendship, both spirits can be nourished, regardless if one is a mentor or not. These kinds of healthy relationships are what need to develop among all Friends, especially keeping in mind not to leave out young Friends as they grow spiritually.

In my experience, I am the only active Friend at my school, the token Quaker, which usually leaves me with no one to talk to about my spiritual findings and leadings. As I continue to develop spiritually I find, more and more, I need other Friends to talk to who are familiar with my struggles. The lack of relationships between adults and young Friends is not only an issue within Durham Friends Meeting, but in meetings across the country. I recognize that there are efforts to improve youth programs everywhere, but it never hurts to start locally. As a graduating senior this year, and as an involved Friend, I plan to work on improving my relationship with my meeting as a whole. I hope also to make way for better relationships between members and young Friends in the future. This, however, needs to be fully a double-sided effort; young Friends need to recognize that they can and need to reach out to the adults in the community, and adult Friends need to recognize that they can and need to reach out to the younger members of the community. We're all on a spiritual journey, and we all have a lot to learn from each other.

Claire Reddy, 18
North Carolina Yearly Meeting (C)
& Piedmont Friends Fellowship, USA

Being a Quaker in the world

In my life I can't tell how much of my influence is from Quakerism, but I do live by the principles of Quakerism. I like that I can have strong different opinions and still be able to talk with people and hang out with them and get to know them. One of the best examples in this area is not using drugs, but still being able to be friends with people who do and have good conversations about both our similarities and differences and life in general.

One of the principles that I follow is that people have made the best decision that they could come to in difficult situations, so people who use drugs were just not able to come up with a better solution for their problems. Pretty much everybody that I know says that they want to quit smoking but now is not the right time because they smoke to get away from other problems that they think are worse. If I can give them another way out, by having conversations and letting them tell me what is going on in their lives, then things can go better for them. Maybe they won't need to do drugs, but even if they do I've given them another thing to think about.

The original reason to not do drugs was that I didn't see any reason to do things that destroyed my mind when I could have fun with people without being under the control of any substance. Now, after having that viewpoint for so long, I feel as though people expect me not to do drugs. I know if I was around many of my friends who do smoke, they wouldn't let me even if I said I wanted to, because they would know that I would not be thinking clearly, and it's not who I am. They want to have somebody in their life who gives them hope that people don't have to end up the way they've been forced to.

I knew that I had an impact on others one night at a party where I believe I was the only person not under the influence of at least one substance. I took a chance there to get to know people, and over the duration of three hours that I spent with two young women, neither of them had another drink. It was good enough to just have a conversation, to just hang out. We talked for a while and took a walk around the neighborhood at 2AM, then sat outside because it was too crazy inside. Since I wasn't drinking it seemed as though they weren't as interested in drinking either. They know that people are stupid when they're drunk, and most people just drink to not be out of the loop. So having somebody who was out of the loop, and fine with it, helps others see the possibilities.

Another place where I've had different thinking is around male training. It seems difficult to spend time with other guys unless the topic is sports or sex. I remember one time at school asking one guy, who was saying how bored he was, what he wanted to do. It was a new idea that he could choose to do something and other people would want to do it with him, no matter how different it was. First he didn't know, then he said he wanted to go outside. Once we were outside he said he wanted to wrestle on the grass, so we did. It was useful to find a new activity and not get stuck in the pattern of what we normally do together (playing basketball or playing cards).

I feel as though I'm kind of challenging life and people in general by not acting the way other people do. I feel weird when I say something to someone I don't know, or when I say hello to someone on the trolley who I've never met before, because I think that other people will judge me. They will look at me funny because I'm acting more freely than they're comfortable with, and will scorn me because they're uncomfortable with the fact that I can do that kind of thing when they would have liked to and were shot down when they originally tried.

I talked to a man on the subway one day and he started telling me about his life. People were looking at me as if I was crazy to be talking with this person who I'd never met before, that it was really weird that he felt comfortable enough to actually be open to me about what was going on. Where everybody has suspicions of everybody, I was breaking the age, class and race barriers, along with the standards of not being social or outgoing to anyone.

I had many feelings about that experience. First of all I felt odd when he started to talk to me, because I was in a mind-set of keeping to myself. Then after I realized that he had something to get off his chest, I felt awkward because other people were looking at me and thinking that I shouldn't be talking with him. Then I felt odd because he felt so comfortable with me and started telling me about all of the different things that were going on in his life, that he was acting human with me. Breaking those barriers and having a real conversation with somebody I'd never met before and probably will never see again was an eye-opening experience for me and something that I'd like to try to do more often. Seeing that the man felt so comfortable with me also helped me realize that people are still interested in human contact even if they aren't already acquainted.

I started playing basketball at the local park about a year ago. I enjoy the game enough that I want to be able to play without having to reserve a court in advance or wait until I go to school the next day. About two months ago I went out with my housemate and we played with a group of about ten other people, all African American. By that point I already knew enough of the people and enough people knew me that I didn't feel that I was out of place as the only white person on the court. The culmination came the day after, when I was riding the trolley home from school and I ran into one of the guys I'd played with the night before. Instead of seeing an intimidating larger black guy who was getting off at the same trolley stop, I just saw another guy that I might play with that evening when I went to the court, and we were able to have a brief conversation and a connection.

The one thing that isn't difficult for me at all around my principles is staying nonviolent. My school community has a code of nonviolent conduct. People understand that it's a strong principle for me, and it's more acceptable to many of my peers than being against drugs or some of the other things that I'm interested in.

Last fall I was at a retreat of the Student Union, a group of high school students from all over the city working together for better schools. We were doing play wrestling, with everybody getting a turn. There was one person who didn't want to wrestle because she wasn't the violent type. Everybody knew that I was the other one who didn't fight – we'd made a strong enough impression just by how we lived our lives. So they all said, "Abby needs to wrestle" and "Andrew jump in!" and pushed both of us into the middle. We sat down on the mats and had a conversation about why fighting was not the solution to the problem, while the others laughed a lot. Then we decided that we were finished and other people went in and had very violent wrestling contests.

These are mainly inner city black folks, some of whom are in the armed forces. It was a contradiction to see the two of us not ready to get into a physical fight. But that difference wasn't a problem in the group. We don't have to butt heads on violence every time we get to see each other, because we have another reason to be together. We get together because we want to reform the school system, not because we want everything about us to be the same. I don't understand why people take one thing they don't have in common with each other and use that as a basis for not having a relationship. It makes sense to me that people can have and find a common belief no matter how many differences there are, and you can base a relationship on that common belief.

Andrew Esser-Haines, 19
Philadelphia Yearly Meeting, USA

London sunset

Milam Smith

On the mission field

There are many challenges to growing up on the mission field, as well as many rewards. When my family first went to Zambia, there was very inconsistent power (sometimes none at all for several weeks), terrible roads, and unstable phone lines. The hospital where my dad works had two generators, a small one that could sustain a good portion of the hospital and a large one that supported the whole mission station. These generators could not be run very much because of the cost of fuel, and so we had to plan on only having power for a few hours a day, if we were lucky. As far as travel was concerned, it took us a full 12-hour day to drive from Lusaka, the capital city, to our home in Mukinge, because the roads were terrible. The phone was too expensive to use, so we relied on e-mail for nearly all of our communication. Even e-mail, however, was inconsistent. Some days the phone line would carry our messages, and some days it wouldn't. If it happened to be one of those days where the computer could connect to the internet, the transaction was so slow it made you wonder if anything was happening at all.

The hardest thing to deal with as a missionary kid (MK) is the time that you are forced to spend away from your family. In today's world, you can't do anything without a good education, and in order to get a good education from Zambia, you have to go to a boarding school. Boarding schools operate on a three-month basis. You spend three months at school, go back home for a month, and return to school for another three months. This means that three quarters of your entire life is spent entirely separated from your home and your parents. This can be very hard on MKs, who are forced to learn at an early age how to adapt to whatever situation they are put in.

Although there seem to be many setbacks for an MK, there are also many blessings. In fact, I would have to say that there are more advantages than disadvantages to being an MK. While I'm home on vacation, there is plenty of space for me to do nearly whatever I want. I used to love making things out of wood, and would braid tree-bark together to make my own rope. Although I never made anything really impressive (I did make a good ladder once), I thought it was a lot of fun. Another of my hobbies is soccer. There are a lot of other kids who live very nearby, and sometimes we go together to the soccer field and kick a soccer ball around. The balls don't always last very long because there are many thorns, but the other kids know people who are very happy to sew the ball back up after it has been punctured.

As far as my spiritual life is concerned, I have many more opportunities to grow in my faith on the mission field than anywhere else on the earth I could imagine. I have seen the Jesus film many times in several different languages, and have seen many people respond to the power of the message it contains. I am continually seeing and hearing of amazing ways in which God has worked to do what has seemed impossible. While at home, I go to a church service every Sunday morning where I can't understand a word, but every Sunday night I go to another service in English where I can worship God and learn more about his word. Sometimes I go with my parents to rural villages where they teach about God and about how to grow in his word. There are many opportunities for me to be a witness at my home. At my school, there are just as many opportunities for community outreach. With roughly five hundred students, mostly MKs, I am given a wide range of topics for personal and group study. My sister and I are the only Quakers there, so we do not get a lot of Quaker influence while at school. It seems to us, though, that the label is not what matters as much as what is on the inside. At our school, each student is challenged to think through what it is they believe and why. The conversations that we have among ourselves are astounding. We have mandatory chapel five days a week and church on Sunday. In addition to these, we can choose among several other worship services and prayer meetings for optional attendance.

God has blessed my life so much because of the mission field. Although it is often exasperating, and sometimes hard, the blessings outweigh the challenges by far. With vast opportunity to praise God in many different ways and grow in him, I could not hope for a more conducive environment for spiritual growth. I cannot imagine what life would be like if my parents had not responded to the urgings of the Holy Spirit, and I am very grateful that they did.

Levi Carter, 17
Western Yearly Meeting, USA
now living in Zambia

The freedom to decide

When people find out that I'm Quaker, there are three general responses: There's the good ol': "Oh, like those people who ran the Underground Railroad? Cool!" And of course: "You mean... your dad is the guy with the weird hat on the Oatmeal box?" And then there's the occasional "Hmmm. That's strange: I didn't think Quakers existed anymore."

Ha, ha, ha. That oatmeal one gets me every time. But seriously, those are basically the things that people say to me. It's fun to be associated with the Underground Railroad, and quite frankly, I enjoy taking credit for it.

Me: Actually, I'm a Quaker.

Friend: You mean like, you ran the Underground Railroad? That's awesome!

Me: Ah, yes, those old days. It was tough, but we lived through it.

Once, my fifth grade teacher was having us correct sentences with spelling and grammatical errors in them, and one of the sentences was this:

> *The Quakers were a religius group who broke away from the Church of England under the leadership of George Fox*

Being a good student, I immediately caught the spelling error in 'religious' and added a period at the end of the sentence. Then I changed 'were' to 'are', correcting the tense of the sentence. When my teacher checked it, she rebuked me for it. I had no response to this; my faith was being challenged. Was I, or was I not, a member of the Religious Society of Friends?

One man actually told me that I wasn't a Quaker. "Do your parents drive?" he asked suspiciously. When I said yes, he said with an air of finality, "Then you can't be a Quaker."

So, in a way, going to a Quaker meeting has always made me different from my friends. "What do Quakers believe?" they always ask, and I have no answer but, "We believe that it is wrong to fight. We believe it is wrong to lie. And we believe it is wrong to do that which you believe is wrong."

At this point, they will exchange glances and then look back at me. "But what do you do when you go to church?" they'll ask, and I'll sigh and tell them that we sit in silence and wait for God to send us an individual message – not through a preacher, but straight to us, which, okay, does sound a little corny next to big Catholic ceremonies and the repetitive, soothing chants of Jewish congregations. Now all of my friends will smirk down at me. "Do you believe in God?" they'll sneer, and I'll have no idea what to say.

You see, my parents have never told me that there is only one truth – I think that's one of the things I like about Quakerism so much. You don't *have* to believe one particular thing. We have no creed that is *for certain exactly undoubtedly* the truth. (Because the truth is different for everyone else, I think – and I'm proud to say I came to that conclusion myself.) *

So now, when someone asks me a generalized question about Quaker beliefs or creeds or ceremony, I simply smile serenely and say, "Tell you what – my meeting has this great pamphlet you should read. Let me get it for you."

So, I enjoy going to meeting, and I enjoy going to Quaker camps. And I like being different. But most of all I like knowing that I have the freedom to decide for myself what I believe, in my family *and* in my meeting.

Anna McCormally, 13
Baltimore Yearly Meeting, USA

* The Quaker understanding of Truth is a complex one. This author expresses a part of it – discovered through her own experience – but not the whole of it. Friends have not traditionally believed that truth is relative, or that it changes over time or from one person to another. Rather, we have believed in continuing revelation, that God continues to reveal Truth (with a capital T) to each person individually, without intermediary. This leads to many different interpretations of Truth, or different personal truths, if you will. However, although Friends believe no one person can know the *entire* Truth, that does not mean that we don't believe absolute Truth exists. The Truth we are all seeking, though it may be expressed and lived in many ways, is universal Truth.

A good Friend

I have not always been a Quaker. For the first eleven years of my life, I was a Methodist, but then my family began attending the Friends Meeting in Portland, Maine. We became gradually more involved there, and I talked with, and learned from, many interesting and wise people, but the one I came to know best was Bob Philbrook. He had had polio when he was a child and was limited in what he could do physically. But he knew a great deal about how things worked and how to repair them if they didn't. Bob was a released Friend, who lobbied at the state legislature, was very involved in American Friends Service Committee (AFSC), and with numerous local committees and groups which worked for causes related to peace, and on criminal and economic justice issues.

One Sunday when I was 14 I was talking with Bob after meeting, and he asked me if I would be willing to work for him in his house and yard from time to time. I was very eager to do this, and so my coming to know him better began. I lived about 45 minutes outside the city, so he had to drive back and forth each time. Working for him was a wonderful thing for me. He taught me to use tools I hadn't used before, and to do electrical repairs, and how to repair gas engines, and many other things. On the drive back and forth we would talk about wide-ranging topics, and I learned a lot from him about how the Quaker testimonies were being applied to current issues in the city and state, and about AFSC and its work. Sometimes he would tell me a scenario and ask what I would do as a Quaker if I were in it. One of them was: you are a relief worker in a small African village, and there is a pregnant woman there who needs medical attention. You try to convince her to go with you to the clinic in the city, but she will only go to the village witch doctor. Do you try to make her go with you, or do you let the situation be? I could not decide what was right, and afterwards Bob told me that he never could either.

When I had been working for him for almost a year he asked me if I would be interested in going to Philadelphia with him to weekend AFSC meetings periodically, because he had to have someone to push his wheelchair, and his wife was tired from doing it very frequently. One day we spent an hour or so practicing with the wheelchair, going up and down over curbs, and through doors, and down sidewalks and across streets until I felt fairly comfortable pushing him and it. The first time I went with him we had a 6AM flight to Philadelphia, so we had to be at the airport by 4AM. I had practiced folding and unfolding the wheelchair so that it could go into the baggage compartment, and everything went fairly smoothly. We got to the Friends Center just in time for the first meeting of his committee. I didn't stay for the meetings that weekend, because they were revising a document word by word, and while I admired their patience, I did not have enough after an hour or so. I walked around the center of Philadelphia, and came back at planned times to push Bob through the meal lines, and out to the hotel at the end of the day. The second weekend when I went with him was a meeting of the Criminal Justice Committee, and I sat in on it. It was very interesting and informative about current conditions in prisons where the members of the committee were working, and two of the people had been closely studying prisons and police in the Mississippi Delta, and told of the degree of corruption and racism which was at work in those systems. I was very interested also to hear what modern-day Quakers were being led to do in regard to these ongoing issues.

Soon after those trips my family and I moved to a Catholic Worker farm in upstate New York, which was what we felt led to do, but was a long way from the people we knew at home. We went back to Maine in September, and I worked with Bob for several days out of the two weeks we were there. I still asked for his advice and received his help the first two years at the farm. He wanted to come out to the farm, and see the place, and bring lumber to make picnic tables, but he never had time. I worked with him each September back in Maine, but in June of 2003 he had a heart attack, and was in the hospital most of the time that summer with complications from it. I went there to visit him that fall when I got back to Maine, but he had had a relapse, and was very ill. He couldn't speak, but I talked to him for a little while, and I believe he knew who I was. He died the next day, and I regret that I knew him for so short a time and that he never made it to the farm, but I am grateful for the time we had. He influenced me in many ways, as a Quaker, and as someone trying to change things for the better. I still hear his voice in my mind from time to time, reminding me of things that he had told me before, and that I kept forgetting over and over. I still forget some of them, but of the people I know, he was the one whom I most aspire to be like, and I will always remember him.

Zachary Hoyt, 17
New England Yearly Meeting, USA
(currently active in New York Yearly Meeting)

Under the shell

There's this girl in my year, who was always alone; I wondered what was on her mind. I knew she was a hard worker and got stressed, but surely that was no excuse to be alone. We tried to be friendly but that never worked, so we got to the point of defeat. Then I noticed this other person emerging who only came out in our free time. I once followed to see where she went, and ended up down the yard. Once through the gate this "new" person appeared as if by chance or fate. I soon came to learn that horses were the answer to getting past the shyness. The next day I asked her, "Do you like horses?" and for the first time a long conversation unfolded. From that day to the present we have been friends and have taken up horses together. I'm glad I cracked the shell after trying for so long, as underneath was this kind, loving and gifted person.

Jennie Evans,
Britain Yearly Meeting

Reflections from the Peace Rally in Washington, DC, January 18, 2003

Today I got my pictures back from the march. I was the photographer: that was my job. It is an outside way of being in. How can you capture half a million faces? The masses cannot be contained in a two dimensional way. I watched the march as an outsider, through a lens of an inanimate object. How could I portray the march, the full effect of being with so many people with similar opinions, without seeming so small myself? Perhaps this was the point. I am only one. Compared to the crowd, I was small. Maybe that is all I could capture, perhaps this is how to give the perception of how large the crowd was. Taking what I could, I depict the march as it was: small groups of people gathering together. Looking at the photos, I wonder. Do these pictures represent what I want to portray? Every photographer asks herself that question. Do these photos speak? They say a picture is worth a thousand words. Are these? Have I captured the essence? That's what it all boils down to. The essence. When the glitz, the extravagance has all been taken away from the 3D nature of the march, and all that is left is the emotions, the need, the pure 2D-flatness of it all, does it still portray what I am trying to say?

To those who have never been to a march, pictures can only attempt to show them what the march was about. The sounds, the voices, the immense nature of the rallying, 3D elements of being, of living, those parts of life that cannot be captured by a camera. The nature of photography is attempting to capture something 3D and give it enough elements – lighting and composition for example – to make it look realistic when there are only two dimensions to reproduce the 3D image. Thousands of cameras spill into the march, hundreds of professionals are there, recording the event. But, even if all of these photographers printed all of their negatives from this march, and put them together in a collage, would they be able to capture what the march was about? Could they show the world what we were trying to say; will they convey the message we wanted the world to hear?

As the photographer, could I take what all the thousands of protesters felt? Or was that not the point. Perhaps all I could capture was what I felt, what I saw. After all, I am only one out of thousands of people. I am just part of the whole; I have my role, but you have yours too. Where will you stand?

Mary Crauderueff, 18
Philadelphia Yearly Meeting, USA

London protest

Milam Smith

Quakerism affects my daily life

Quaker teachings have answered most of my doubts about life and currently I am obliged to live and behave as a Quaker.

When I was five years old I had an extraordinary experience. My cousin died and was buried the following day. I asked my parents what had really happened to him only to be informed that he had died! "What is death?" was my next question. Then I asked a more challenging question – when was he coming back from the grave? Their answer to these questions was: his life had gone to God, his body was rotting in the grave and he will never come back. However, this did not satisfy my mind. If they buried my cousin as he was, then was the grave the God they were telling me about? They insisted that life left the body and went to God and what was buried was only the body. On several occasions when my parents were not around I used to go to the grave and call him by name hoping he would hear me and come back. This experience introduced me to the understanding that when one dies the body is for the grave and the life is for God. Further, the separation of the life from the body leads to death.

During Sunday school I was introduced to God as our Father of Life. For God made humans in his own image. After God made man he breathed his spirit into him. Every human being is in a form of life that takes up God's likeness and by this claim God wants us to dedicate our lives to him. So my search about life and God continued until I was introduced to George Fox. In learning about Quakerism a satisfactory answer was found. "For in every man there is that of God" is the consciousness that commands us to differentiate between what is good and bad, condemns you guilty when you do wrong, has its own laws and debates about what one has to do.

The body acts on these commands. God is love and this consciousness of God in every man is acceptable to God and reflected in all who adhere to God's will and commands. This was revealed by his son Jesus Christ in his commandment "Love each other as I have loved you" (*John* 15:12) and "you are my friends if you do what I command you" (*John* 15:14). Based on this search for truth in my everyday life I seek to measure up to the expectations that God binds me to – basing my life on the golden rule and Quakerism. So I have to act by conforming to these demands of God and my faith as a Quaker.

My speculations today are:

- I am here

- I really do exist

- If the earth existed for millions years ago before I was born where was I?

- Thinking about 100 years from today 99.9 percent of the population existing in the world today, including myself, will not be around, so where will we/I have gone?

- If I have power to do what my conscience (life) directs me to do now, will it blow out like a candle to a state of nonexistence?

- If after life ends a person vanishes, what then is the purpose of life?

This draws me to the experience of different types of deaths. I call you to your similar experiences as we begin to imagine of what type of life conditions we are likely to be in after death.

Imagine someone locked in a house that is set on fire. He will struggle until the life (conscience) leaves the body and the body becomes loyal to the fire. Whether it is burnt to ashes or rescued, it no longer offers resistance.

The second experience is if someone is drowned in water. He also struggles until the life escapes from the body. The body then turns loyal to the water, whether it floats, sinks, or is eaten by water creatures, it offers no resistance.

The third experience is someone ambushed by thugs and either beaten or shot to death. At first he will struggle but immediately after the life escapes from the body, it will then become loyal to the torture and it offers no resistance.

So from the above experiences and any other experiences we may add, we confirm/prove that the body is already at home. In a peaceful or normal death it will be buried or it will perish in fire and it has no objection. The biggest and most challenging idea to think about twice, or thrice, and much deeper is – in what place and under what conditions does this resister (life) to all death situations need to be in? Further the doubts about whether there is continuity of life after death is resolved. Life merely escapes from the body to the next world for continuity in a better place than that where the body is laid to rest.

As a member of the Quaker church we should appreciate God for the inspiration revealed to us through his son Jesus Christ and the inspired search for God by George Fox. Thus Quakerism confirms for us that each one of us has "that of God," always assisted by the Holy Spirit so that our bodies may portray God's glory in preparation for staying with God in his glory for eternity when we leave this world.

Nakhumitsa Doris, 18
Uganda Friends Church

Graveyard

Sonja Kincaid

A Friendly Perspective

(This article first appeared in the May 2005 issue of Quaker Life.*)*

I was born a birthright Quaker in Whittier (as in John Greenleaf Whittier, mind you), California, to Quaker parents. I was raised at Whittier First Friends Meeting until I was seven. My family then moved to Richmond, Indiana, a veritable Quaker enclave with three meetings for worship and Earlham College, and we became members of West Richmond Friends Meeting, which has worship services in the programmed tradition.

I attended meeting faithfully, went to Sunday school and, when I was old enough, attended middle and high school young Friends groups regularly. I went to senior high camp at Quaker Haven, participated in youth programs of Indiana Yearly Meeting sessions for years, attended Ambassadors for Christ in Washington, DC, when I was a high school sophomore, and celebrated my 19th birthday at YouthQuake in Seattle, Washington.

When the time came, I applied and was accepted to Friends-affiliated Earlham College. But I wanted to get away from Indiana so I chose Beloit College in Wisconsin, where there are only a handful of Quaker students and no structured Quaker community on campus. There is a small unprogrammed meeting only a block away from my college dorm, but I went only once. The Sabbath has truly become the day to rest. And rest. And rest some more.

As a child, I was a pretty good Quaker, I guess; I struggled with practical nonviolence (I have a younger sister) but I was all about honesty and integrity. Once my sister and I disobeyed the house rules and ordered a pizza to be delivered when our parents were away. We would have gotten away with it too, if it weren't for my conscience. As soon as my parents got home, I wrapped my arms around my mother's legs, sobbingly confessed my guilt and showed her where we had hidden the empty pizza box.

I don't know what to tell you about what it is to be a young Friend now. Things aren't as simple as they used to be. There are bigger things to worry the soul than the issues of forbidden pizza delivery.

Our country is enmeshed in a messy, unnecessary war. The factions of our government quarrel bitterly amongst themselves. The citizens of the United States are constantly lied to and coached to be fearful by their government representatives and the members of the media. People my age must face the fact that we, our peers, our brothers and our sisters, are being asked to trust our government – a government that barely half of us elected to serve – and support a war, sometimes to the point of going to fight and die in a country that didn't want us there in the first place. We worry about the recall of the draft and about our futures in this time of bloody conflict and political uncertainty.

I am concerned about the touting of "moral values" over actual intelligent and compassionate governance, but I certainly can't speak for all young Friends. In fact, I'm not sure I'm adequately equipped to speak for myself. Where am I now on the road to spiritual fulfillment? A deluxe rest stop. I don't go to meeting when I'm at college, and I rarely go to meeting when I'm home for break. I'm too old now for most young Friends gatherings, with the exception of the World Gathering of Young Friends, and too young to get excited about yearly meeting business sessions or monthly meeting luncheons.

Once a Quaker by faith, practice and socialization, I am now a Quaker by name, profession and political identity. I introduce myself as a Quaker; I speak of the basic tenets of our faith and the examples of bravery and love from our history. I can explain the difference between programmed and unprogrammed meeting for worship. I talk about the Light within, George Fox, the origin of the word "Quaker" and the verse from which we got our name, "the Society of Friends." I mention abolition, fair treatment of Native Americans, prison visitation and conscientious objection. I explain that it's not all about Quaker Oats, funny hats or plain speech. I am full of facts but not spiritual conviction. My identity as a Quaker is tied up in my identity as a young Democrat and as a student at a left-leaning liberal arts college.

And what do I do now for Quakers since I don't go to meeting or attend gatherings? Instead of attending meeting, I go to peace protests in Madison, Wisconsin and shout slogans and wave my posters aloft. Peace marches are hardly ever peaceful. Even though there may not be any actual physical violence committed, the air is typically thick with betrayal and righteous wrath. Armed with our indignation, the marchers stomp down Madison's State Street to the capitol building, our eyes flashing and voices hoarse. We hold our paint-spattered posters high until our arms ache. We shout and we stomp and we curse the names of those we believe have wronged us. We dare anyone to disagree. These protests make all those involved edgy and tense and anything but peaceful.

And my strongest Quaker affiliation? I work for *Quaker Life*. My duties include writing up wedding, birth and death announcements, and slicing, dicing and reassembling press releases. I look at heartfelt testimonials with unsympathetic eyes and squeeze them dry, chopping them for content and length. Taking the raw materials I am given, I mold them into my own little emotionless Frankensteinian monsters that totter around on legs of fairly good grammar and terse sentence structure.

Thankfully, many young Friends are not like me, not shallow or cold. Many of my Quaker friends go to meeting (even monthly meeting!) regularly, attend College Young Friends or similar groups, and are actively pursuing ministry and mission work. They are on track and would make any of our predecessors proud. They represent the young Friends who know their direction in life and know that God is with them.

As for me, I represent those young Friends caught in spiritual limbo. We've had the benefit of our Quaker upbringing, we've grown up with the values and beliefs and we have the basic moral structure; now we must decide what to do with it. Will we let our identity erode into a threadbare ideological and political identity? Or will our faith revive as we graduate from college to find a spiritual community of our own choosing? Will we pick careers where honesty, simplicity, equality and peace are valued or will we lose our ideals in pursuit of the almighty dollar or worldly accolades?

Being a birthright Quaker, I tend to take the faith for granted and tend not to work very hard to cultivate it. It's somewhat like being left-handed, unusual and sometimes inconvenient, but I was born this way. I don't ponder the spiritual ramifications of being left-handed. Perhaps it is arrogance or merely apathy, but rather than experiencing a spiritual crisis, I am in a spiritual doldrums, drifting along quite comfortably. In most testimonials, the structure is threefold: the "before," the "crisis", and the "after." In the before, the person confesses how wrong she had been, how she stumbled and faltered and failed. The crisis is the event that changes everything, that wakes the person up and causes the life shift. The after is the revelation, the healing, the part where the confessor discovers or rediscovers faith and her life becomes better, more fulfilling.

I suspect that I am on the cusp of crisis, that I have been spiritually complacent for a long enough time that a shake-up is in order. Maybe not this week, this month or even this year, but almost certainly after graduation and during the all important, post-college job search. What will happen when the sheltering brick buildings of Beloit are left behind and my proud little spiritual dinghy runs aground on a foreign shore? Will I collapse on my own and, realizing my need, cry out, "God help me?" I don't know.

What I do know is that I admire those people who seem to know their purpose from birth, who set out with confidence that God is with them, lighting every stone in their path. I feel like I'm wearing wraparound sunglasses and have a little flashlight that only illuminates the ground at my feet. But I also feel that God is waiting on the path ahead of me, holding a lamp and a box of matches and saying, "As soon as you're ready, I'll light my lamp and you'll be able to see better. Just let me know when you're ready to see." And that's very comforting.

Kerensa Edinger, 20
Indiana Yearly Meeting, USA

EPILOGUE

My hopes for the future/Quakers will rule the world

I hope it will be good.

S'pose it'd be kinda cool if the trees overthrew everything and once mile-high skyscrapers became rubble grew grown into dense forest... weird.

My future looks good. I am convinced I will have a job involving some noticeable level of creativity, and have wife and children etc etc etc bla bla bla. But what I really hope for, and what I won't stop aiming for... is a white piano... with a curved, and VERY colourful keyboard, 'cause that'd be cool. There will be a new species of tree that spits out litres and kilolitres of ozone miles into the sky, regenerating the ozone layer. There will be a type of ant that sucks pollution from the air like a vacuum cleaner.

The future is bright, but the future is NOT orange, because orange is not a colour that one thinks of as entirely natural. QUAKERS WILL RULE THE EARTH... equally of course... along with non Quakers... of course, no, scrap that last bit. Quakers will be a respected rarity, and hearing "Oooh, you're a Quaker!" will still be a lovely thing to hear.

Back to me, I would love to be an artist – either a jazz pianist, or a painter, or a woodcut maker, or a screen-writer, or an actor, or a novelist, or a journalist, or a comedian or a ... or a... a nice person who does nice stuff. ANY profession involving being nice and doing nice things will suit me fine. A country home in northern Italy with cypress trees and orange juice would also not go down badly. A spring and a lake and a king, and a cake and a wing and a dish of fresh black olives under a checked umbrella would be lovely. I would bask like an old tom cat under Italian skies and spend my days being creative and spend my money on things that made the world happy. Quakerly.

Andrew Phethean
Britain Yearly Meeting

Acknowledgements

This book has truly been the result of the Spirit working through many people, each of whom breathed life into this book and kept it moving forward. There are so many people who saw the great potential in creating a forum for young Friends' voices and contributed in whatever way they could to make this book the volume you hold in your hands. This list couldn't possibly be exhaustive and we want to give a nod to those who won't make it into this list: thank you.

We want to thank the young Friends who served on the panel at the QUIP Annual Meeting in Greensboro, North Carolina, in 2002 that inspired us to initiate this project, for having the courage to speak their Truth. They were Simon Gray, James Barnard, and Sara Barnard, all from Great Britain, Elizabeth Baltaro and Martin Kelley. Sara Barnard deserves a special mention for first suggesting an anthology of young people's writing about Quakerism.

Elizabeth Cave has been a tireless and enthusiastic supporter of this project. She encouraged Mina Temple to take the idea forward at Britain Yearly Meeting's Junior Yearly Meeting in 2003, where writing workshops took place. She has read the submissions thoroughly, served as an advocate for the project on Britain Yearly Meeting's publications board, and worked to the very end, proofreading the final pages.

Rachel Daniel and Hana Turner Uaandja brought a lively report on the process at the QUIP Annual Meeting Woodbrooke (2003), together with some samples of writing whose quality persuaded us the project was worth pursuing.

Barbara Mays has shepherded this forward with great enthusiasm from the beginning, writing the original call for submissions, developing a lesson plan for youth workers, sending out the call for submissions as far as she could reach. She has kept the light shining on this project and stayed up late with us the night we chose selections for the book. She's lent her editorial expertise along the way and for her steady faith in this book, we thank her.

Trish Carn has been a faithful supporter and tireless worker on this project. She compiled submissions into a document so that we could easily read them without knowing the authors' names, and has communicated regularly with the publications board of Britain Yearly Meeting about the progress of the project. Lastly, Trish graciously volunteered her time and talents as designer on this book, despite tight time constraints and a lot of committee consultation on the cover.

We owe a debt of gratitude to Lucy Duncan, for her excellent work soliciting submissions, gathering together an editorial board, and keeping the whole process moving along, as well as attending to a host of small editorial details that no one else seemed to have time for. We're not sure how she had time for them either, since she was simultaneously working a demanding job and caring for a young child. If not for her dedication, diligence and enthusiasm, this book would not have happened, or at least, not yet.

We thank Barbara Hirshkowitz and Peter Daniels, who cared for this book as publications managers for FGC and Britain Yearly Meeting. We additionally thank Barbara for copy-editing the manuscript, working with the printer, and promoting the book.

We thank Donna Neff from Evangelical Friends International for sending us three Publishers of Truth essay contest volumes quickly, so we could consider them.

We are very grateful to Twin Rocks Conference Center for providing the fine beach house in which we met. It was lovely and refreshing and looking out onto the orange sun setting over the ocean helped to keep our work centered.

We thank Graham Garner for finding some fine restaurants near the beach house, so we could sustain our strength through all the hard work we did the weekend we met.

And, lastly, we want to thank Zion for bringing the Frisbee.

Author/Artist/Editor Biographies

These passages have been written over several years. Many of the writers are of an age where people move around frequently. We have traced all we can to ask them about themselves.

W. Geoffrey Black (Editor, 'The schism chart') is 18 and lives with his family on 60 acres in western Wisconsin. He has been both home-schooled and a Quaker his entire life. The smallness of his monthly meeting, and the lack of other teenagers, has led him to be very involved with Northern Yearly Meeting's teen program and to attend regional and national teen gatherings, as well as the 2004 Quaker Youth Pilgrimage. His interests include writing, religion, traveling, and mechanical typewriters.

Natasha Bullock-Rest ('Early stages of love'), 17, is on the staff of her school's literary magazine. She has an obese cat, Lipstick, and a penchant for humorous British literature. She enjoys dancing with her friends and listening to Belle and Sebastian.

Randy Burns ('Facing the fear factor'), 12, attends North Shore Friends Church in Houston,.Texas.

Levi Carter ('On the mission field') is a 17-year-old missionary kid who has lived more of his life in Africa than in the United States. He says, "I accepted Jesus Christ as my personal Lord and Savior at a young age, and have continued to grow in him ever since." His parents were called back to the mission field from Indiana, where he was born, arriving in Zambia on Levi's tenth birthday. As well as attending other schools and doing some home-schooling he has attended the Rift Valley Academy, an American Christian boarding school in Kenya. After he graduates, he is looking forward to finding out what the Lord will call him to do.

Cait Caulfield ('I felt God'), 17, is from Fairbanks, Alaska, but currently living in Shanghai, China, on a year-long exchange program. She is a member of Chena Ridge Monthly Meeting and an avid attender of FGC's Gathering. Her passions are reading, theatre, and languages/linguistics. She hopes somehow to combine them at college next year.

Mary Crauderueff ('God in nature,' 'Finding my roots,' 'Reflections on the Peace Rally'), 18, is a first-year student at Earlham College. She is from Philadelphia Yearly Meeting and she went to YouthQuake 2003.

Hayo Daniella ('God can speak to each of us') a 15-year-old Burundian Friend, is a member of Kamenge Friends Church in Bujumbura. She is the granddaughter of one of the first Quakers in Central Africa.

Kerensa Edinger ('A Friendly perspective'), 20, is an editorial intern for *Quaker Life*. She is studying in Quito, Ecuador, in a Beloit College exchange term. She is a member of Indiana Yearly Meeting.

Andrew Esser-Haines ('Being a Quaker in the world'), 19, is a member of Central Philadelphia Monthly Meeting and just completed his first year at Earlham College.

Lucy Entwistle ('The Quaker Youth Pilgrimage'), 17, was born in Beverley (UK) in 1988. She comes from a Quaker family and is active in Young Friends' events, both in Yorkshire and nationally. She is currently studying for her A-levels and hopes to go on to take maths at university. Her likes includes Frisbee and eating drumstick lollies but she dislikes her nose and animals with beards.

Jennie Evans ('Under the shell') has just finished her A levels at Sidcot School (a Quaker boarding school). She plans to do a course on small animal care.

Levi Fletcher ('Tough times'), 12, is a member of a Friends Church in Newberg, Oregon.

Alison Freeman ('The richest 3%'), 17, is an attender who tries to live her life by Quaker principles. She says, "I have a strong social conscience and am vociferous about my vision of the world, which should be based on love and sustainability, not profit!" She has a just finished an International Baccalaureate. Her teenage years have been very active, interweaving spirituality with everyday life.

Richard George ('My Quaker journey'), 15 (13 when he wrote his essay), attends the Charter High School for Architecture and Design in Philadelphia, after studying at Frankford Friends School. At twelve years old, Richard joined Frankford Friends Meeting, with the support of his family. He helps out with First Day School. Richard's faith and social consciousness are strengthened through his attendance at the Young Friends of Philadelphia Yearly Meeting. He is an avid sports fan and enjoys playing for the Frankford baseball team.

Elisabeth Grabowski ('Quaker camp'), 14, was born in Romania where her birth mother put her and her sister up for adoption. She says, "She wanted us to be adopted so we could have a better place to live, because she was so poor. In the orphanage at 14 months in my cold and rusty cot, I saw a lovely, kind, and caring couple. I put my hands between the bars of my cot and pulled on the lady's skirt.That lady is now my superb mum and her husband is now my fantastic dad. Being adopted is the best thing that could have happened to me. I'm going back to Romania to find my birth mother." Her favourite school courses are drama and textiles."

Dot Greaves ('Where I stand with Quakerism'), 19 (17 when she wrote her piece), was born and grew up in Wales with her large family. She is just finishing her first year of a geology degree at Oxford. She says, "My one definite aim is that whatever I end up doing, I am going to travel everywhere. I want to see the whole world!"

Jennifer Gulliver ('Me'), 18, (16 when she wrote her piece) lives in Ayrshire in Scotland. She plays the flute and the trombone and likes doing gymnastics. She has just finished doing herA levels at Ackworth School (a Quaker boarding school) and wants to go to Cambridge University to study maths in autumn 2005.

Sakinah Afiyah Hassan ('Quaker school', 'Quakers: equality'), 15 (13 when she wrote the essays), loves writing, especially poetry. She studies music and plays the flute and piano. She says, "Quakerism is a part of my life and I feel very secure within the community. I can go to many Quaker events and be able to relax and be myself – away from the harsh lifestyle of the world we live in today!"

Owen Hayden ('It's only a game'), 14, lives in Amherst, Massachusetts with his family. He participates in young Friends' activities sponsored jointly by Mt. Toby Friends Meeting and Northampton Friends Meeting.

Laura Herring ('In a Quaker Meeting') attended Junior Meeting of Britain Yearly Meeting in 2003.

Daniel W. T. Hood ('From the silence'), 16, is a drama student in Greensboro, NC. He attends Friendship Meeting regularly, and New Garden Meeting and First Friends Meeting occasionally. His mother, Sarabeth Terrell, is a recorded Friends minister and has always been an integral part of his religious upbringing. He writes poetry.

Lauren Hoy ('Just silence'), 14, lives in Vienna, Virginia, where she attends Rachel Carson Middle School.

Zachary Hoyt ('A good Friend'), 19 (17 when he wrote his essay), is an associate member of Portland Friends Meeting. He has spent the last four years at St. Francis Farm, a community in the Catholic Worker tradition in northern New York state. He is involved in the Alternatives to Violence Program. He enjoys playing the guitar, accordion and tenor recorder, as well as building instruments including moutain dulcimers and a hammered dulcimer. He is interested in learning to live in a more sustainable and sane manner.

Sonja Kincaid ('Graveyard' drawing), 18, attends Wilmington Friends Meeting, Ohio. She has received several awards for her works of art.

P. Zion Klos (Editor, photo), 18, says, "I am a positive minded teenager with a zest for life and the natural world." Zion is a member of Fox Valley Friends Meeting (Northern Yearly Meeting) in Wisconsin. He has a passion for Frisbee and plans to attend Colorado College in the fall.

Lawrence McManamy ('God alone,' 'Nonviolence'), 13, has always lived in Newburyport, Massachusetts. He attends New England Yearly Meeting in the summer and the Junior High meeting retreats throughout the year. He discovered Thomas Hazard III (1720-1798) when investigating his Quaker genealogy. He says, "I've been a Quaker my whole life, and it is a large part of who I am."

Anna McCormally ('The freedom to decide'), 13, She lives in Herndon, Virginia, and enjoys Tae Kwon Do and Ninja turtles.

Daniel Murphy ('I open my eyes'), 14, attends Herndon Friends Meeting in Virginia. He is a student at South Lakes High School and is pursuing the International Baccalaureate program there.

Nakhumitsa Doris ('Quakerism affects my everyday life'), 19, was born in the village of Sikomosi in the Mbale district of eastern Uganda to Quaker parents. She joined the church Sunday school at the age of three, then began attending the adult gathering at age 11. She has assisted with Sunday school and is the church choir leader. She likes to share the word of God with friends. She is taking Higher School Certificate and is looking forward to attending university.

Meg Nelson ('YouthQuake'), 16, is a high school student who lives in Illinois. She is a member of Upper Fox Valley Quaker Meeting and is a co-clerk for Illinois Yearly Meeting High School Friends. Her family often provide inspiration for her writing and critique it. Her two cats, Benjamin and Luke, keep her and the family company. She enjoys spending time outdoors with nature and loves bike riding, mountain climbing and running. Someday she hopes to publish her own book.

Andrew Phethean ('My hopes for the future/Quakers will rule the world'),19 (17 when he wrote this) is a university student in Scotland.

Catherine Playfair ('What Quakerism means to me'), 17, was born in London and moved to Leicester when she was 15. She met Quakers at her new school and she "was almost immediately drawn to the idea of silent meetings. I went to one meeting and felt so welcomed and comfortable that I was very eager to become a member of the community and involve myself in the practical activities. Since then I have joined the outreach committee. I really enjoy all aspects of Quakerism and look forward to future projects I can be involved in."

Lily Press ('I hear God singing within me'), 16, is a member of her school tennis team. She plays harp in several local symphonies and orchestras, and as a freelance musician.

She hopes to study writing, music and literature at college. She says, "Since I was five, I have been a voracious reader, and this has naturally led to an interest in writing."

Claire Reddy (Editor, 'A healthy addiction,' 'The Importance of Friendship between Adult and Young Friends,' two photographs), 18, is a member of Durham Friends Meeting. She has been an active participant in the high school program at the FGC Gathering and FGC's Young Quakes conference. She plans to major in chemistry or biochemistry at Wellesley College. Quakerism and science are the things with which she involves herself with passion.

Brianna Richardson ('Encircling silence', 'Silence,' 'Candles,' and 'A query'), 18, is a member of Bellingham Friends Meeting. She helps take care of the youngest children in her meeting. She has recently developed a leading for writing – poetry in particular – and has since coordinated writers' retreats for her peers, where young writers work in a productive atmosphere, forming an active support group for sharing their work. Brianna plays viola and especially enjoys chamber music. This fall sheplans to study music and English at the University of Puget Sound.

Erika Marie Richter ('Silence?'), 17, is an active participant in Poplar Ridge Friends Meeting of New York Yearly Meeting. She is involved with the meeting's youth activities and works for peace in her community. Recent efforts have included petitions, speeches, and the Books not Bombs protest. The meeting family at Poplar Ridge brings her strength and solace as she continues to work to find her place in the world.

Aliyah Shanti ('There is a Spirit'), 17, is a student at Smith in Massachusetts, majoring in music composition. She is amember of Olympia (Washington) Friends Meeting and an active sojourning Friend at Northampton Friends Meeting.

In December 2004 – January 2005, she went to south India to help with tsunami relief efforts and, with the assistance of Olympia and Northampton Friends, returned in the summer of 2005. She is an award-winng poet and composer and has sung with the Leaveners in London, UK.

Milam Smith (Editor, cover photograph, other photographs throughout the book), 15, is a member of Stevens Point Monthly Meeting of Northern Yearly Meeting. He enjoys photography, playing video games, programming and being sarcastic. Dressing gruesomely is also a hobby.

Rachel Stacy (Editor, 'My Journey to Faith'), 19, is a first year student at Earlham College. She plans on majoring in Chemistry and religion. She plans to travel abroad and meet other people and other Quakers. She hopes to work toward the unification of Friends across the world. She supports her spiritual and religious exploration with her involvement a varity of Quaker activites ranging from working with Earlham College's Quaker community, to helping plan the World Gathering of Young Friends 2005.

Aubrey Stanton ('Whispers'), 13, loves writing and has been attending Herndon Friends Meeting for over six years.

Taylor Stanton ('The tingle of God'), 16, is a junior at Fauquier High School. She loves writing and also has been attending Herndon Friends Meeting for over six years.

Calvin Alvin Taylor, III ('Talking with God'), 16, attends enjoys reading, mostly science fiction and fantasy. Besides Virginia, he has lived in Louisiana, Texas and Oklahoma.

Charlotte Thomas ('Prayer'), 15, has been a Quaker for nearly ten years. She says, "Quakerism has always been a large part of my life, becoming of increasing value in recent years as I have matured and come to a more coherent understanding of my spirituality." She enjoys making music, reading, socializing, and studying languages, mathematics and religion.

Trillian Turner ('Praise be to God!' 'Self-Portrait'), 19, is a member of North Seattle Friends Church. She attended Kiev National Conservatory in Ukraine and Bellevue Community College this past year, and hopes to continue her schooling at George Fox University in Newberg, Oregon. She plays piano and double bass and also loves to write and draw. But her favorite activity is playing ultimate Frisbee, especially in the mud!

Mica Whitney ('Shadows'), 15, was born and raised in Richmond, Virginia and is active in the youth programs of Richmond Monthly Meeting and Baltimore Yearly Meeting. At school she focuses on literary arts. Her interests include playing the guitar and writing. She hopes to pursue a career in writing fiction and creative non-fiction.

Michael Wild ('Simplicity'), 19 (17 when he wrote his essay), grew up in London. "My father moved to the United Kingdom from Zimbabwe before I was born. When I was eight, he took a year off work here and took me to live with some family there." Michael took some time off to earn money after sixth form, which allowed him to take part in conservation and teaching projects in Belize and Guatemala. He also traveled around Mexico for a while. He will soon finish his first year in a philosophy course at the University of York.

QUIP
UAKERS UNITING IN PUBLICATIONS

This book project and QUIP (Quakers Uniting in Publications)

At the 2002 QUIP annual meeting in Greensboro, North Carolina young Friends from Britain Yearly Meeting gave a presentation about their spiritual journeys. Moved by the vitality and spirit of those young Friends, the meeting minuted two decisions: 1) to offer a platform for young Friends to share their faith experiences more widely in a book written and edited by young Friends and 2) to set aside money in the budget to make it possible for young Friends to attend each QUIP annual meeting. Trish Carn, Lucy Duncan, and Barbara Mays, with the help of many other committed QUIP members and Friends, have worked as the project coordinators for this book from the inception. It has been an engaging and elucidating process for those who have worked with the editorial board and for QUIP as a whole.

What is QUIP and what is its work?

Begun informally in 1983 by a small group of Quaker publishers and booksellers, QUIP is now an international organization of 50 Friends organizations and many individuals concerned with the ministry of the written word. Members currently work together to achieve common goals:

- A website listing of all Quaker publications currently available at www.quaker.org/quip.

- A website promotion of recent books by member Quaker authors and publishers at quaker.org/quip.

- Cooperative marketing.

- Accessible centers for distribution of Quaker publications.

- Cooperative publishing.

- A forum for exchange of editorial concerns.

- Annual meetings for education, business, and encouragement of faith.

- An increased awareness of Quaker publications in the broader religious book market.

- Opportunities for introducing the wider public to Quakerism.

- Tacey Sowle Fund grants to aid Third World Friends in publishing and distributing Quaker titles.

For more information about QUIP and its activities, contact Liz Yeats, administrator, at quip@2quakers.net. You can find the membership materials at www.quaker.org/quip.